A Brewery in Bedford
The Charles Wells story

Roger Protz

A Brewery in Bedford was first published in 2005 by Charles Wells Ltd, Eagle
Brewery, Havelock Street, Bedford, MK40 4LU.
Telephone 01234 272766
Email postmaster@charleswells.co.uk
Website www.charleswells.co.uk

ISBN 0-9549401-0-5

Designed by Rob Howells

Printed by WS Bookwell, Finland.

The author wishes to thank members of the Wells family, directors, employees,
former employees and public house tenants and managers who gave
generously of their time and memories.

The author and Charles Wells Ltd acknowledge the enormous contribution
made by Ken Page of the Brewery History Society, whose original research and
drafts made the production of this book possible.

Endpapers: Tom Wells, Joanna Wells and Mike Wells canoeing on the River Ouse
by the Horne Lane Brewery in 1967.

Contents

Today before yesterday

CHARLES WELLS IN THE TWENTY-FIRST CENTURY SEEMS superficially to be a long way removed from the humble brewery established in 1875. The modern company produces amounts of beer undreamt of in the 19th century, much of it in the form of a style called lager that was unknown in Bedford at the time. Some of the beers made today have their origins in the Caribbean, India and Japan, while Wells's own brands are sold in twenty-three countries, including France, Italy, the United States and Russia. It all seems light years away from a small brewery set up to supply a handful of pubs in Bedford and the surrounding towns and villages.

But there is a powerful link that binds old and new. Charles Wells remains a family-owned company run by descendants of the founder who share his passion for quality, honesty of purpose, fair and generous treatment of employees, and success built on ethics rather than the pursuit of quick profit. Charles Wells may today enjoy an international reputation for its beer but the family directors are first and foremost men of Bedfordshire, proud of their roots, their history, and their large estate of community pubs.

The industry in which Wells now operates has changed out of all recognition. When Charles Wells first fired his mash tuns and coppers, much of Britain's beer was still made by publicans in the cellars of their pubs. The tied house system of pubs directly owned and supplied by brewers was in its infancy. With the exception of Burton pale ales and Guinness stout from Ireland, which made use of the new railway system to move beer round the country, there were few national brands. Brewers made beer to suit local tastes and local pubs. When Wells employed the railway to sell beer as far away as Cambridge – an hour's drive today – the company was considered daringly innovative.

Since the 1960s, regional and family brewers have had to operate in an increasingly harsh and competitive environment. National brewers have been created through mergers and takeovers to sell lagers and keg beers that enjoy the benefit of expensive and often memorable advertising. The number of breweries has fallen dramatically over the past 40 years as many companies found it difficult and even impossible to survive. Some forty-four breweries

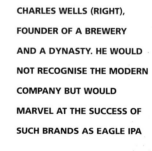

CHARLES WELLS (RIGHT), FOUNDER OF A BREWERY AND A DYNASTY. HE WOULD NOT RECOGNISE THE MODERN COMPANY BUT WOULD MARVEL AT THE SUCCESS OF SUCH BRANDS AS EAGLE IPA

closed in the 1990s, many of them famous and even much-loved independents. Today the top four brewing groups account for eight out of ten pints of beer brewed in Britain. Many of the surviving independents have battened down the hatches to concentrate on supplying their own pubs and the local free trade. Charles Wells could have 'down-sized' by closing the Eagle Brewery and moving to a smaller green field site. But the directors accepted the challenge of using their large brewing plant to expand rather than quietly decline. The expansion has been driven by a growing demand for Wells' own beers, an export policy that is unique among independent brewers, and contract brewing for companies of world renown.

Export drive

In 1997, when Charles Wells received the Queen's Award for Export, it was recognition of an initiative that had at first been viewed with scepticism by not only the rest of the brewing industry but also by many within the company, who looked on the quest for overseas sales as 'the chairman's hobby'. In the early 1980s, the board had taken up the call by the government to 'export or die', when Prime Minister Margaret Thatcher argued that companies should boost their profits from selling abroad. John Wells said a brewery based on a tied estate of pubs within a 60-mile radius of the brewery couldn't hope to compete or survive in the growing global marketplace. His first step was to put Bombardier premium bitter into bottles and offer six-packs of the beer to the United States. That first tentative step failed but John Wells was determined to confound his critics within and without the brewery. He spoke to representatives of the large Italian community in Bedford who said there could be an important niche in the beer market in Italy for strong English ales. Young Italians, famous for their awareness of style and fashion – *la bella figura* – were breaking free from the shackles of their wine-drinking elders and were anxious to try new drinks. At first the going was tough. Wells had to learn about the nature of a quite different retailing culture, based on loans to bar owners. There is intense rivalry between bars and Wells soon discovered that appointing one national distributor handling outlets in the same town or street wouldn't work as it reflected badly on individual bar owner's machismo. When Wells

appointed several distributors in the 1990s, sales of its beer started to take off in Italy.

Exporting beer is part of a culture at Charles Wells known as 'permission to fail'. Wells dares to innovate, try new strategies and even new markets on the understanding that some initiatives will fail but most will succeed. Today Wells's exports account for 22 per cent of production. When it bought the John Bull overseas pub chain from Allied Domecq it acquired outlets in Russia and the Baltic States. It's a remarkable success story. In the past, only national brewers, Bass and Guinness in particular, have bothered to export to countries where lager is the mainstream style. Charles Wells has introduced English ale to a vast audience that would otherwise never come into contact with the style.

The business has grown in other and equally unusual ways. When Horne Lane closed and was replaced with the new brewery in Havelock Street, capacity was increased and by 1990 the new brewery had doubled in size at a cost of £35 million of borrowings. It was a brave commitment, one that, with the benefit of hindsight, might not have been undertaken if the directors had been aware of cataclysmic events in the 1990s that were to turn the brewing industry and pub trades on their head. Blissfully unaware of the problems that lay ahead, in 1976 the key consideration was to maximise the use of the splendid new brewery that, using the most up-to-date technology of the day, could produce ale and lager in the same vessels.

THE EXPANSION HAS BEEN DRIVEN

BY A GROWING DEMAND FOR

WELLS'S OWN BEERS, AN EXPORT

POLICY THAT IS UNIQUE AMONG

INDEPENDENT BREWERS,

AND CONTRACT BREWING FOR

COMPANIES OF WORLD RENOWN

The early success of Havelock Street was the result of two quite separate developments: the Campaign for Real Ale, formed in 1971, had had a profound impact on the brewing industry by rekindling a demand from consumers for naturally-conditioned cask beers; at the same time, other consumers who were enjoying the first fruits of overseas package holidays had developed a passion for colder lager beers. The Eagle Brewery was able to meet these disparate demands by increasing both the quality and consistency of its draught ales, and by signing a contract to brew Red Stripe lager. It was the success of Red Stripe that drove the new site and enabled the company to take on other contracts with overseas brewers, but it was a success that came at a price and with many sleepless nights.

Red Stripe is a Jamaican beer that was first brewed in 1938 by Desnoes & Geddes of Kingston. People from the Caribbean who settled in Britain after World War Two retained fond memories of the beer, one they passed on to the next generation. D&G saw a potential for sales in Britain and held talks with Whitbread in the 1970s about producing Red Stripe under licence. Whitbread said the proposed volumes were too small and suggested the Kingston brewery should approach Charles Wells. It was an exciting challenge for Wells: it would not only help to boost volumes at the new brewery but would also enable technical director Roy Morewood to prove the

The Charles Wells family tree

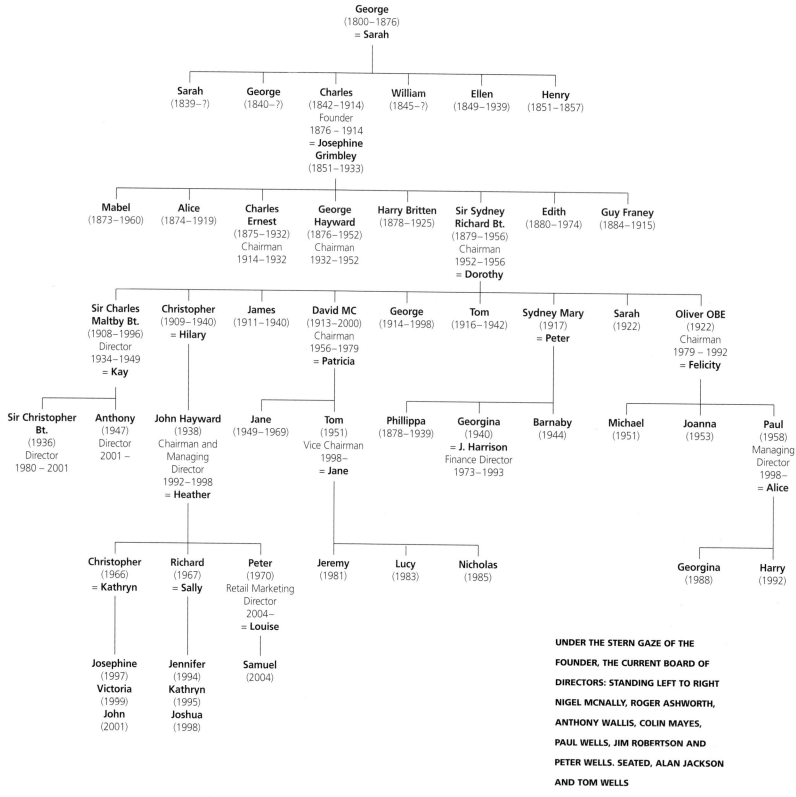

George
(1800–1876)
= **Sarah**

Sarah
(1839–?)

George
(1840–?)

Charles
(1842–1914)
Founder
1876 – 1914
= **Josephine
Grimbley**
(1851–1933)

William
(1845–?)

Ellen
(1849–1939)

Henry
(1851–1857)

Mabel
(1873–1960)

Alice
(1874–1919)

**Charles
Ernest**
(1875–1932)
Chairman
1914–1932

**George
Hayward**
(1876–1952)
Chairman
1932–1952

Harry Britten
(1878–1925)

**Sir Sydney
Richard Bt.**
(1879–1956)
Chairman
1952–1956
= **Dorothy**

Edith
(1880–1974)

Guy Franey
(1884–1915)

**Sir Charles
Maltby Bt.**
(1908–1996)
Director
1934–1949
= **Kay**

Christopher
(1909–1940)
= **Hilary**

James
(1911–1940)

David MC
(1913–2000)
Chairman
1956–1979
= **Patricia**

George
(1914–1998)

Tom
(1916–1942)

Sydney Mary
(1917)
= **Peter**

Sarah
(1922)

Oliver OBE
(1922)
Chairman
1979 – 1992
= **Felicity**

**Sir Christopher
Bt.**
(1936)
Director
1980 – 2001

Anthony
(1947)
Director
2001 –

John Hayward
(1938)
Chairman and
Managing
Director
1992–1998
= **Heather**

Jane
(1949–1969)

Tom
(1951)
Vice Chairman
1998–
= **Jane**

Phillippa
(1878–1939)

Georgina
(1940)
= **J. Harrison**
Finance Director
1973–1993

Barnaby
(1944)

Michael
(1951)

Joanna
(1953)

Paul
(1958)
Managing
Director
1998–
= **Alice**

Christopher
(1966)
= **Kathryn**

Richard
(1967)
= **Sally**

Peter
(1970)
Retail Marketing
Director
2004–
= **Louise**

Jeremy
(1981)

Lucy
(1983)

Nicholas
(1985)

Georgina
(1988)

Harry
(1992)

Josephine
(1997)
Victoria
(1999)
John
(2001)

Jennifer
(1994)
Kathryn
(1995)
Joshua
(1998)

Samuel
(2004)

UNDER THE STERN GAZE OF THE
FOUNDER, THE CURRENT BOARD OF
DIRECTORS: STANDING LEFT TO RIGHT
NIGEL MCNALLY, ROGER ASHWORTH,
ANTHONY WALLIS, COLIN MAYES,
PAUL WELLS, JIM ROBERTSON AND
PETER WELLS. SEATED, ALAN JACKSON
AND TOM WELLS

flexibility of a plant that could produce lager beers that included other cereals and brewing 'adjuncts' in their composition as well as traditional barley malt.

The arrangement with Desnoes & Geddes created a British company, Red Stripe Marketing, which was owned equally by the Jamaican company and Charles Wells. Bulmers of Hereford handled distribution of the brand. Bulmers was best known as a cider manufacturer but it had also built a nationwide drinks distribution system and seemed the ideal partner for Wells. At first Red Stripe was a startling success, with volumes peaking at 130,000 barrels a year. Bulmers forecast that Red Stripe would continue to increase sales in the 1990s and it was this optimism that encouraged the directors of Charles Wells to commission a second brewhouse in 1991 to cope with demand. To their consternation, sales of Red

Stripe started to decline at the same time as the impact of new government rules for the industry started to take effect. In 1989, a report by the Monopolies & Mergers Commission into the industry was highly critical of the 'complex monopoly' exercised by the national brewers which, the report said, kept beer prices artificially high and restricted smaller brewers from getting a fair access to market. In the wake of the report, the government introduced the Beer Orders that instructed the nationals to sell substantial numbers of pubs to bolster the free trade, and to permit their tenants to take guest cask ales free of the tie. The turmoil that followed did not give the independent sector the increase in sales they had anticipated. The national brewers started to sell their retail outlets to new pub companies. Many were created with financial help from the brewers and were run by senior managers who left the breweries to run the pub companies. As the pubs were not required by the Beer Orders to take guest beers, they naturally restricted their choice to generously discounted beers and lagers from the nationals.

While the impact of the Beer Orders did not have a major effect on Charles Wells's fortunes – and the company has since built a substantial presence in the national free trade – the Bedford brewery, in common with all smaller brewers, was hit by the arrival in the early 1990s of the 'open borders' policy introduced by the European Union. As British beer is highly taxed while in mainland Europe it enjoys low rates of duty, vast amounts of cheap Belgian and French beer were imported into Britain at a rate estimated to equal the annual output of two of the bigger regional breweries in this country. A large proportion of the imported beer is bootleg, sold at car boot sales and other informal markets, including in some cases pub car parks. The result was a sharp decline in sales of heavily taxed British beer sold through pubs. Charles Wells was the victim of a triple blow: an unexpected fall in sales of Red Stripe, upheaval in the pub trade, and cheap foreign beer flooding into the country for home consumption. The manner in which the company reacted to this unprecedented challenge would determine the success or failure of the brewery in the 1990s and the new century.

'Own label' scramble

The priority was to fill the vessels in the enlarged brewery. Charles Wells embarked on a policy of producing 'own label' beers for supermarkets and other major retailers. The problem with own label – beers that carry the name of the retailer rather than the producer – is that they are marginal profit products. It's a good business to be in if volumes are high. But in the 1990s, as beer sales slumped as a result of the rising tide of cheap imports from mainland Europe, the national brewers joined the scramble to make own label beers. They were able to utilise their large plants to produce volumes of beer beyond

THE MISTS OF TIME...OFFICE WORKERS AND THE GATEMAN OUTSIDE THE ENTRANCE TO THE BREWERY YARD AROUND 1902

the capabilities of smaller brewers such as Charles Wells. As a result, Wells found its income from the own label business falling alarmingly as the supermarkets cut prices in a bid to compete with bootleg beer, and were demanding ruinously deep discounts from their suppliers.

At a strategy meeting of the board in January 1998, the view held was that the own label plan was seriously harming the company. Two-fifths of the brewery's annual production was devoted to own label and the board took the decision to exit from that market. The new course meant building Charles Wells's own brands beyond the local market, seeking new beers to brew under licence, and to restore the fortunes of the Red Stripe brand.

Red Stripe's success was critical as, at its peak, it accounted for 92% of the brewery's volumes outside the tied estate. But the distribution agreement with Bulmers meant that sales and marketing control lay elsewhere and volumes continued to decline alarmingly, throwing Wells's calculations and forecast into doubt.

Negotiations began for a new agreement and, in the meantime, attention turned to the other brands in the portfolio. In 1993 the Kirin Brewery in Japan had granted the

rights for production and sales of its Kirin Lager brand to Wells and, while sales had not been dramatic, they had grown well and created good margins. With the addition of the Kirin Ichiban premium beer, sales began to rise and marketing was given a bigger investment.

Wells had approached the European office of Grupo Modelo in 1997 with a view to taking on the distribution of the Corona Extra lager brand. The contract at the time was with Whitbread but sales were less than 100,000 cases a year and Wells convinced Modelo it could improve on that figure. As a result, a plan was launched with a joint sales and marketing team with Eurocermex, the Modelo subsidiary in Europe, and seven years later sales broke through the two million case barrier.

Eventually the contract with Bulmers was mutually and amicably terminated. This enabled Wells to take over responsibility for sales, marketing and distribution of Red Stripe. This was fortuitous, for in 2003 Bulmers went into a deep and terminal financial crisis that ended with the world's most famous cider maker being sold to Scottish & Newcastle. It had been a long partnership with Bulmers, stretching over 20 years, but the pressure on margins in the British beer

A STEAM TRUCK OUTSIDE THE BREWERY OFFICES AT HAVELOCK STREET. THE TRUCKS REPLACED HORSES EARLY IN THE 20TH CENTURY

business took its toll in the last five years.

Charles Wells had to prove to the satisfaction of Desnoes & Geddes that it could handle sales of Red Stripe. The international drinks group Diageo, better known as Guinness, controlled more than 60% of D&G. Wells had to show that it had the marketing muscle to succeed, otherwise it ran the risk of losing the brand to Diageo, with its own formidable sales force.

Success in the beer market for Bombardier, Kirin and Corona helped win the day, but the major proof that Wells could successfully handle sales and marketing came from Red Stripe itself, for since taking over the brand, Wells has seen sales of the brand grow once more. By 2003, Bedford was brewing 100,000 barrels a year and it's expected that the brand will once again hit a peak of more than 200,000. Red Stripe's sales are divided between 70 per cent packaged and 30 per cent draught. It's available nationally through the take-home market and is increasingly in demand in the pub companies' national outlets as well as in Wells' own pubs. The success of Red Stripe not only appeased Diageo but also enabled Wells to build on that success by signing contracts to brew the Indian lager Cobra.

Pub programme

Charles Wells has not ignored its core businesses: ale and pubs. Draught ale still accounts for 53 per cent of production and the tied estate of 254 pubs offers enormous advantages for direct sales. A large investment programme has been launched to refurbish pubs and bring them up the standards expected by consumers in the 21st century. Wells admits it is fortunate in having a substantial number of its pubs in attractive rural locations. But whether in towns or villages, all the pubs must offer the creature comforts of a decent pint, a genuine welcome from the staff, and comfortable seating. On this bedrock, restaurants, wine and good food have been added in suitable houses. Above all, Wells's tenants and managers have to listen to their customers and respond to their needs. As one director puts it, pubs used to happen by accident, now they happen by design. Training and certification for tenants and managers is considered essential. Wells introduced training schemes in the late 1970s and now works closely with the British Institute of Innkeeping to run courses either in the new Eagle Centre at Bedford, built at a cost of £1.5 million, or at BII venues. Tenants, who make up the vast proportion of the people directing Wells's pubs (there are only 17 managers), have a career structure designed by the company, which views them as entrepreneurs who need to run pubs as good businesses.

Charles Wells also accepted the challenge of building sales of its ales, Bombardier in particular, in the free trade. Its sales team has focused on the new national pub companies and has made sure that tenants and managers in those pubs know how to order Wells' beers. The company has invested heavily in creating a bigger sales team whose members are trained and skilled in more than just selling but can help or advise with the installation of dispense equipment and cellar temperatures. The core belief of the sales team is that a guest beer can become a regular beer if all aspects of sales are good: efficient supply, quality of product, ease of handling, point-of-sale material, and reliable after-sales attention. The company has carefully monitored the new pub companies to see which ones would make good partners.

Wells has refused to go down the road of deep discounting of beers to the pub companies and has built up good relations

CHARLES WELLS HAS INVESTED

HEAVILY IN A BIGGER SALES TEAM

WHOSE MEMBERS ARE TRAINED IN

HELPING WITH DISPENSE SYSTEMS

AND CELLAR TEMPERATURES

SOME OF CHARLES WELLS'S
MODERN RANGE OF BEERS,
INCLUDING SEASONAL
ALES AND LAGERS BREWED
UNDER LICENCE

with Enterprise Inns, Unique Pub Company, and Pubmaster. The challenges of the modern on-trade can be gauged by the fact that in 2003 Pubmaster was taken over by Punch Taverns, Enterprise and Unique plan to merge, while SFI has bought the Slug & Lettuce pub group. In spite of the continual turmoil in the free trade, however, Wells has managed to build sales of Bombardier to the point where it's now one of the leading premium cask beers in Britain. It's now the eighth biggest brand and its market position improved during 2004 as a result of tireless work by the sales team.

Beer at home

On the back of the surge in sales of the draught product, Wells has introduced Bombardier in bottled form to exploit a sector of the take-home trade that is growing by more than 10 per cent a year. The company has also developed the mini cask, an attractive silver container shaped like a beer cask that contains eight pints of real ale. Like a pub cask, the beer needs to settle to allow the sediment to drop to the foot of the container, but the beer is easy to handle and serve, and brings the pleasures of live beer to drinkers at home.

Bombardier now enjoys twice the sales of Eagle Bitter, though Eagle remains the leading brand in Wells's own pubs.

Research carried out by Charles Wells has shown that consumers prefer beer produced by a family company to products made by national brewers in 'beer factories'. Wells has underscored its independence and fresh approach to marketing by promoting Bombardier as the beer to drink on St George's Day. The company was prompted to launch a national promotion for St George's Day when it found that St Patrick's Day had become one of the major annual events in the English pub trade calendar, mainly to the benefit of Guinness and other Irish brewers. Using the red cross of St George was a hazardous path to tread: it could have conjured up images of the less appealing side of modern football as well as the activities of far-right racist groups. But Wells distanced itself from such extremes by using its campaign to call for a national holiday on 23 April, which also happens to be William Shakespeare's birthday. It has proved highly successful, giving Wells a national image it had

never before enjoyed and further boosting sales of Bombardier. The company has also looked at its range of ales and has introduced new seasonal beers. One new product, Banana Bread Beer, has proved particularly successful. Its soft, creamy, less bitter character appeals to drinkers who normally avoid traditional hoppy ales, and it was voted the most popular beer among women drinkers at the 2003 CAMRA Great British Beer Festival.

2003 was a momentous year for Charles Wells. Profits of £3.8 million were the best for several years. And the company was awarded the prestigious Regional Brewer of the Year award in March by the weekly trade newspaper, Publican. It was recognition of Wells's standing in the industry and the manner in which directors, management and staff had remodelled the business in the space of a few short years. It is now reliant on beers it either owns or which are brewed under contract with long-standing and reputable brewers. Mark Stretton, chairman of the judges and Publican's city and business editor, said in his citation: 'Charles Wells has transformed itself from a low margin, own label brewing business into an innovative, brand-focused, sales-driven

company. Reasons for winning included the triumph of Bombardier, commitment to its customers and dedication to its people.'

There has been a subtle change in branding: the brewery's own beers are now labelled simply Wells. This should not be seen as an attempt to dump the past but as a need in the modern, fast-changing brewing industry and pub trade for easily assimilated brand names and images. This book is recognition of the fact that all at Charles Wells are proud of the company's past and its enduring traditions. In common with many firms, Wells has not always been careful with its history. Much of it – records, plans, photographs, prints, advertising material – went into skips when Horne Lane closed. This history has had to be painstakingly teased out, with much material gained from private sources. Now we can tell the whole story. Having painted a picture of the company, successful and vigorous, at the beginning of a new century, it is time to go back to Victorian times to unravel the fascinating story of the origins and development of a brewery in Bedford.

The Cross Keys, Pulloxhill
Peter Meads

Peter Meads has run the Cross Keys at Pulloxhill for more than 30 years and has seen customers' demands change out of all recognition. Twenty years ago he used to sell 15 gallons of sherry a week but that trade has almost completely disappeared. He has also seen the disappearance of early morning trade, when farm workers would come into the pub for a drink at 9.30.

The Cross Keys dates from the 17th century and was owned by the Ampthill Brewery until it was bought by Charles Wells in 1886. Peter says he used to serve people who lived and worked in the area, but now many villagers commute to London. They don't have local roots and if they come to the pub they tend to leave early as they have to be up and out the following morning to get to work.

Peter has always served meals at the pub. In his early days he would sell 300 meals on a Saturday. He offered just a main course and dessert and would have three sittings. He now serves full meals in a 50-seat restaurant. He has always offered a special lunchtime menu for retired people.

His main complaint about modern trading is the red tape. He spends ten hours a week tackling paperwork and has to handle legal matters and VAT, while he finds fire officers and environmental health officers 'very demanding'.

Peter's beer sales are now split 50:50 between ale and lager. He is a dedicated Charles Wells publican. Both his sons were born in the Cross Keys and he has helped to train other tenants.

Home is the sailor, home from the sea

IT'S THE STUFF OF WHICH SOAP OPERAS ARE MADE: Charles Wells gave up a successful seafaring career and settled down in his home town of Bedford to launch a brewing dynasty...for the love of a woman. While he was on leave in the early 1870s he fell in love with Josephine Grimbly from Banbury in Oxfordshire. Josephine's father approved of the match but – and these were the strict Victorian times of the late 19th century – he said he would give permission for his daughter to marry Charles only if the young man of 30 retired from the Merchant Navy and found a new career that was less dangerous and kept him at home.

In spite of his love for Josephine, Charles must have turned his back on the sea with some reluctance, for he seemed destined for high office and success. He was born in Bedford in 1842. When he left the Commercial School at the age of 14 he was determined to become a sailor. In 1856 he joined the frigate Devonshire as a midshipman and sailed on her from London to India. He was promoted rapidly and was a chief officer by 1868. The Devonshire was owned by a shipping company called Wigrams, and Charles subsequently sailed on three more of their ships, the Kent, the Sussex and the True Briton. He also served on another of Wigrams' ship that took troops to India to put down the Mutiny of 1857-8. Charles was in Australia during the Gold Rush but decided not seek his

fortune by joining the prospectors. He was a diligent seaman, gained his Extra Master's Certificate, and was qualified to serve on steam as well as sailing ships. With the rank of captain, he was offered the command of Wigrams' first steam ship. But then came a spot of leave and a fateful meeting with Josephine Grimbly.

It was not surprising that Charles Wells, forced to seek a new career, went into business. His father George Wells (1800-1876) had built a successful furnishing concern in Bedford. George was the son of Thomas Wells (1775-1857), a basket manufacturer and rush grower who may have supplied rush matting to the House of Commons. Thomas moved to Bedford from St Neots at the turn of the 19th century and in 1839 rented Fenlake Barns as the family home from William Whitbread, a member of the great brewing family. There are no precise records, but it's thought Thomas carried on his trade in premises close to the Rose Inn in Bedford High Street. When he died, his son George moved from Fenlake Barns to Rothsay Gardens in a fashionable area of Bedford. He had

CHARLES WELLS PICTURED AS A YOUNG MIDSHIPMAN AROUND 1852. HIS MARINER'S TELESCOPE (ABOVE) IS STILL ON VIEW AT THE BREWERY

already established his furnishing company at 25 High Street, and by 1869 he had been joined by his elder son, also called George. The substantial business was described in trade advertisements as 'George Wells & Son, bazaar, general furnisher, carpets, cabinet manufacturer, upholsterers, piano tuning, van owner etc'. It seemed that father and son could turn their hands to almost any trade or skill. George Wells junior expanded the business, occupying 23 to 25 High Street and he added a large warehousing facility in Castle Lane. When he retired in 1905 the business continued as Wells & Company and by 1940 had become Wells of Bedford, with 27 High Street added to the store. The successors, Harrison Gibson, traded on the premises until 2000.

The Wells family enjoyed commercial success and a good reputation in Bedford. Charles had married Josephine in 1872 and, while there is no record of what he did for the next three years, there seems little doubt that he turned his mind to which trade to take up in the town. In 1875, the Horne Lane Brewery was put up for sale. Charles, aged 34, saw the potential to carve out a name for himself in an industry that was expanding rapidly to meet the demands of both a burgeoning working class, and a new and well-educated middle class. Bedford, in common with all towns and cities in the late 19th century, was bursting with pubs. Rudimentary beer houses slaked the thirsts of people engaged in hard manual labour. Those in more genteel professions enjoyed a quiet drink in the more salubrious surroundings of the saloon bar as more modern pubs were built.

County town with a proud history and famous sons

Bedford is the ancient capital of the county of Bedfordshire. It stands on the Great Ouse, a river that has proved vital to the town's industries down the centuries, helping to move coal and grain for the coal merchants and brewers in the town, many of whom were involved in both trades.

Bedford was awarded charter status in 1166 by Henry II. The modern borough of Bedford, which includes the town, the urban area of Kempston and 43 villages, has a population of 140,000 and is one of the most culturally diverse areas of Britain, with 57 ethnic groups represented. It is most famous as the home to a large Italian community, which was established in the 1930s when refugees from Mussolini's dictatorship settled in the area.

The best-known son of Bedford is John Bunyan, who is commemorated by a statue in the town. Bunyan was born in Elstow a few miles outside the town. He wrote his most famous book, The Pilgrim's Progress, while he was imprisoned in the county jail for refusing to recognise the established church.

A stained-glass window marking the publication of The Pilgrim's Progress in 1678 can be seen in the Bunyan Meeting Free Church in Mill Street. A postcard image of the window was sent to Terry Waite when he was held hostage in Beirut. Every June, the town hosts the John Bunyan Festival.

John Howard is another famous Bedfordian who also went to prison for his views. He was a Nonconformist landowner in the 18th century who was jailed for denouncing the appalling conditions in the town's prison and the even worse conditions on prison ships. He has a bust in the town and his work lives on with the Howard League for Penal Reform.

The Bedford reformist tradition was continued by Bishop Trevor Huddleston, who was born in the town in 1913. He worked among the poor in London's East End before devoting his ministry to Africa, where he was an outspoken critic of apartheid in South Africa. A statue in his honour was unveiled in Silver Street in 2000 by the first president of a free South Africa, Nelson Mandela.

Sir William Harpur left his mark on the town with the Harpur Schools. He was born at the turn of the 16th century and became Lord Mayor of London. He founded his school in the town, which is maintained by an endowment based on the income from property in London.

Another and more surprising man with a bronze bust in the Corn Exchange is the American bandleader Glenn Miller. His military orchestra was based in Bedford during World War Two.

JOHN BUNYAN'S STATUE IN BEDFORD.

HE IS THE TOWN'S MOST FAMOUS SON

A PROCESSION TO CELEBRATE THE CORONATION OF EDWARD VII PASSES WELLS & CO'S BAZAAR IN BEDFORD HIGH STREET ON JULY 11, 1902

Until the 19th century and the new technologies made possible by the Industrial Revolution, brewing in Bedford, in common with the rest of the country, was largely carried on by publicans on their own premises. The invention in the early 18th century of a new type of beer called porter rapidly transformed the brewing industry. Porter, so named as a result of its popularity with street market porters in London, was a strong, dark and heavily hopped beer, the forerunner of today's stout. The craze for porter, at a time when towns and cities were expanding rapidly as agricultural workers left the land to work in factories, was so insatiable that new breweries sprang up to meet the clamour. The ability of brewers to meet that demand was made possible by such crucial developments as cast-iron and copper brewing vessels, which replaced wooden ones and were able to retain heat more efficiently, and steam engines that provided power to all areas of a brewery. Thermometers and hydrometers measured the temperature and strength of beer, while coke replaced wood as the fuel for drying and curing barley malt. The ability to more closely control the curing (gentle roasting) of malt made it possible to replace brown malt with a paler version: pale malt contains a far higher level of the natural enzymes that convert starch into fermentable sugar during the brewing process. Brewing became a more stable and controllable activity, and also a more profitable one as the better utilisation of malt and hops made production cheaper. Of equal importance, the ability to keep the brewing processes cool by early forms of

Sam Whitbread

One of the earliest brewers of porter in London was Samuel Whitbread, the son a Bedfordshire farmer. He retained close links with Bedford and the county. He had made his fortune from brewing, lived in fine style on an estate in Bedfordshire, had his portrait painted by Gainsborough, and represented Bedford in Parliament.

refrigeration meant brewing ceased to be a seasonal activity and could continue all year round.

By the 19th century there were some nine commercial or 'common' brewers operating in Bedford. The Horne Lane Brewery enjoyed a good position in the town, alongside the River Ouse with wharves where malt and hops could be unloaded and beer dispatched. There had been a maltings on the site since the 18th century. It had previously been a coal merchants owned by Battison's, who were prominent in the coal trade in Bedford. Riverside sites for coal merchants were in demand once the Ouse had been made navigable as far as the Wash in the late 17th century. In 1818 the site was bought by Stephen Benson. He was described as a wool stapler, but he built the original brewhouse some time prior to 1836, pulling down cottages in the process. In 1836 William Johnson, a brewer from Bishops Stortford, and Charles Redden, a draper

from Newport Pagnell, bought the brewery and an adjoining coal wharf. Johnson died in 1848 and Redden became the sole owner. When he, too, died, his widow sold the brewery to Joseph Piggott and a Henry Wells from Chelmsford who was unrelated to the Wells family of Bedford. His connection with the town was short-lived as Piggott bought him out in 1862.

Impressive site

When Piggott put the business up for sale in 1876 it comprised a 20-quarter malt house, residence, garden, and paddock of nearly two acres, a five-quarter brewery powered by a horsewheel and 35 public houses. Buildings and brewing equipment included a loading store, beer store, yeast room, tun room and brewhouse, a five-quarter mash tun, iron liquor back that held 50 barrels, a 13-barrel open copper with iron wort back, hop and under backs, coolers, refrigerator, pumps, pipes and cocks, horsewheel, machinery and gear. The coal wharf was included in the site. (A quarter was a form of measuring weight and was short for a quarter of a hundredweight or 28 pounds. This equals approximately 14 kilos in modern measurement.) It was an impressive site for its time, making use of many of the new industrial developments of the 19th century. The 35 pubs included 11 in Bedford, 20 in the surrounding county, one in Northamptonshire and three in Buckinghamshire.

Piggott's brewery was put on the market on 18 December 1875 and the auction was fully reported in the Bedfordshire

THE HORNE LANE BREWERY

ENJOYED A GOOD POSITION IN

THE TOWN, ALONGSIDE THE

RIVER OUSE, WHERE BEER

AND MALT COULD BE LOADED

1883
April 9

Times. An experienced brewery auctioneer, Alfred Thomas of London Bridge, said the average annual beer trade for the past three years had been approximately 3,500 barrels. When the sale started, Mr Smail of Sharman & Smail, the solicitors acting for Charles Wells, made the first bid of £10,000. Bidding slowly rose to £16,000. Charles had the financial support of his father and the promise of a personal loan of £12,000. We can only imagine the tension he suffered as the bidding rose and he wondered whether he would lose the opportunity to own his own business. When the sum of £16,500 was reached, the auctioneer told the meeting: 'Mr Piggott had left the amount in my hands, and if there was no advance he would sell at £16,500. ' Mr Smail, on behalf of Charles, then bid £16,700. After a long pause, which must had added immeasurably to Charles' nervousness, the business was sold to Mr Smail.

The personal loan of £12,000 came from a Thomas Wood. There are no records of him, but it is believed he was a private investor in Bedford. His investment proved to be a safe one.

Charles Wells threw himself with enormous vigour and enthusiasm into running and building the trade of his brewery. As a former sea captain, he had sound experience in managing men. In naval terms, he was also determined to run a 'tight ship' and avoid getting into debt. His original capital was £20,391 and in his first year in business he made a creditable profit of £829. He sold off the adjoining coal business in 1878 in order to concentrate on brewing. Two years later he expelled a family of pigs from the premises: at that time it was the custom to keep pigs in breweries that ate the spent grain at the end of the mashing cycle. A new cellar and stores were added, and in the first four years of his ownership trade increased from 3,229 barrels to 5,632. Six additional pubs were bought and in February 1880 Charles' capital had increased to £30,500.

Bolstered by this rapid success, Charles set about expanding the business. In 1881 he bought nine pubs for £4,486 at an auction at the Swan Hotel in Bedford. The pubs came from the 28-strong estate of Henry Fowler of Woburn Brewery. The Fenny Stratford Times reported that Henry Fowler was now an inmate of a lunatic asylum, not a fate that befell many

AN EARLY EXAMPLE (ABOVE) OF BEER FOR HOME CONSUMPTION. BELOW, A DIARY FROM 1883 RECORDING THE DIGGING OF AN ARTESIAN WELL TO SUPPLY VITAL BREWING 'LIQUOR' TO THE BREWERY

Artesian Well

Tools arrived 9 am
Men do 11.20 am
t Crab up on platform, and own Men
ing out earth down to Gravel 10 ft from
urface
Down to rock 14 feet from Surface
Struck fault in rock, Blue Gault about
17 feet from Surface
wenty feet from top of Tube no allowance for dirt

1883

May 19 of rock and then in Clay a
19 Took out about Six feet of Cl
21 In Clay 66 feet from Surface,
4 inches of Clay and about One
25 Eleven o'clock am On hard lim
105 feet from Surface,
lower rod, waiting for Crows
30 Through about Two feet of Rock
up in Clay Samples 108 fe

23

THE OLD AND THE NEW...THE WHEATSHEAF AT
BOW BRICKHILL AROUND 1890 (LEFT) AND THE
MODERN VERSION OF THE SAME PUB, ABOVE

brewers. Charles Wells, being of sound mind and financial acumen, prudently borrowed £3,500 in 1882 and a further £1,000 a year from Thomas Barnard, a banker with offices in Bedford High Street, conveniently close to the bridge and the brewery: the loans were speedily paid off. With his capital increased to £41,250, Charles set about rebuilding the brewery. A new tun room, where beer was matured before leaving the brewery, was built in 1882, and other parts of the site were altered during the course of the next three years to cope with rising demand for Wells's ales. A new maltings was added in 1887 at a cost of £3,000. Annual production had risen to close to 10,000 barrels and the capital employed increased to £52,000. As a result, Charles was able to pay off £6,000 of the loan from Thomas Wood. The outstanding balance was cleared by 1889.

Charles took the opportunity to not only rebuild parts of the brewery but also to improve the Brewery House and offices. His wife, Josephine, was offered the choice of a riverside view or one facing Horne Lane. Surprisingly, she chose the street as her outlook. The house was completed and paid for in 1884. Her husband's business continued to expand briskly. By 1890 the brewery owned 80 pubs and enjoyed an annual trade of 12,552 barrels. Capital increased to £70,000. A new brick chimney, which became a prominent site in the town, was built in 1892 and new stores, stables and offices were added. The tied estate became more widespread. By 1893 Charles had bought two pubs each in Cambridge and Luton. As horse-drawn transport was still used for local deliveries, it is likely that beer was sent by train to both towns, which had direct rail links with Bedford. Railway draymen would have finished the journey to the pubs.

St Peter's Brewery in Lurke Street was opened in 1813 by Nathaniel Wells Small, a corn dealer and maltster. St Peter's never developed a strong pub estate and concentrated on beer for the take-home trade. In 1878 the brewery was bought by Frederick Charles Fuller from Essex, who renamed it the Bedford Brewery. He enlarged the site, enabling production to triple in size. Fuller introduced jars of beer with taps for consumption at home. Charles Wells bought the brewery and three pubs in 1934 for £12,500. The site was demolished, and the land was sold and used to extend the car park of the newly-built Granada cinema. As a result of the purchase, Charles Wells acquired the title of the Bedford Brewery; Fuller's brass

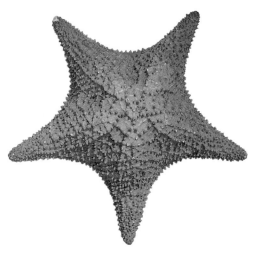

THE STARFISH LOGO WAS USED BY CHARLES WELLS FOR DECADES ON PUBS AND BOTTLES UNTIL IT WAS REPLACED BY THE EAGLE MOTIF

Other Bedford breweries in the 19th century

St Paul's Brewery

St Paul's Brewery dated from 1666. In 1803 it was sold to William Long, later Sir William, who died in 1841. His grandson, Bingham Newland, became the sole owner of the brewery and 29 pubs. When he died in 1873, the business was put up for auction. Thomas Jarvis was the successful bidder. He paid £29,650 for the brewery and 28 pubs, plus a further £4,550 for seven pubs owned separately by Bingham Newland. Jarvis sold the site to The Harpur Trust in 1876 to enable it to enlarge its grammar school. Part of the present Town Hall now occupies the site.

The Phoenix Brewery

The Phoenix Brewery, built in 1867 in Midland Road, was also owned by Thomas Jarvis, who had been a brewer and maltster in Bedford for several years. He became one of the leading brewers in Bedford, acquiring the St Paul's business and building a 37 strong estate of pubs. When he retired in 1883 the business of Ale & Porter Brewers, Maltsters, Wine and Spirit Merchants was continued by his three sons who

THE WHITE HORSE PUB OWNED BY THE JARVIS BREWERY IN MIDLAND ROAD, BEDFORD.

IF YOU WANT TO GET AHEAD, GET A HAT...
EMPLOYEES AT THE CASTLE BREWERY IN 1895.

acted as partners of Jarvis & Co. They added mineral water to brewing and built a new factory for its production alongside the brewery. Walter Jarvis became the sole proprietor of the company but when he died in 1915 his nephew Talbot was away on military service. The business, worth 10,000 barrels a year, was put in the hands of a receiver and was sold to Charles Wells for £79,000. Brewing stopped on the site in 1918 and the premises were sold to Munton & Baker, who adapted it to produce malt extract. When Colonel Talbot Jarvis returned from the war in 1920 he joined Charles Wells to manage their pub estate. The family connection continues to this day, with Jarvis Solutions, Charles Wells's specialist packaging division, based alongside the brewery.

St Mary's Brewery

St Mary's Brewery opened in 1783 by the river bridge on St Mary's Street. It was owned by Peregrine Nash and the business was run by his

descendants as Nash & Co. The business did well and in 1874 the Nashes drew up plans for a new steam brewery at Lurke Street. As a result, St Mary's Brewery was demolished in 1876.

Lurke Street Brewery

The Lurke Street Brewery opened in 1875 and, promoted as a steam brewery, clearly made full use of the modern technology of the day. When the owner, William Joseph Nash, died in 1884, his sons were already dead. Susan Nash, his 75 year-old widow, was left to run the business with her five daughters. In 1890 she went into partnership with William Pritzler Newland, owner of the Duck Mill Brewery, and brother of Bingham Newland. Mrs Nash owned 62 pubs with a capital of £12,000 while Newland owned 13 pubs worth £600. Duck Mill had been opened between 1872 and 1873 by Frederick Thomas Young, a former manager of St Paul's Brewery. Young over-extended himself as a result of buying the Old Sun Brewery at Eaton

Socon and several pubs. In 1874 he went into partnership with William Pritzler Newland, but the partnership was dissolved in 1876 and Newland became the sole owner. When he formed his partnership with Susan Nash, the smaller Duck Mill site was sold. Newland & Nash at Lurke Street flourished and became the second biggest brewery in Bedford after Charles Wells. Breweries in Northill and Potton were bought. The company was sold to Wells & Winch of Biggleswade (no relation to Charles Wells). The last brew was made in 1924 and all production was transferred to Biggleswade; the brewery was bought by Greene King in 1961.

Castle Brewery

The Castle Brewery was built in 1838 by Charles Higgins, the publican of the Swan Inn in Bedford. He leased land at Castle Close from the Duke of Bedford at a rent of five shillings a year. The company was subsequently run by Higgins's sons and their descendants. In the 1920s, the owners Lawrence and Cecil Higgins both wanted to move away from Bedford and sold the business in 1927 to Wells & Winch. Trade was around 12,000 barrels a year. Cecil Higgins's collection of china, glass and furniture was left to found a museum in the town.

St Peter's Brewery

St Peter's Brewery in Lurke Street was opened in 1813 by Nathaniel Wells Small, a corn dealer and maltster. St Peter's never developed a strong pub estate and concentrated on beer for the take-home trade. In 1878 the brewery was bought by Frederick Charles Fuller from Essex, who renamed it the Bedford  Brewery. He enlarged the site, enabling production to triple in size. Charles Wells bought the brewery and three pubs in 1934 for £12,500. Fuller's brass plate (above) is now outside the entrance to the Eagle Brewery.

plate was kept and is now outside the entrance to the Eagle Brewery. Bottled beer was first recorded in 1893. Commercial glass blowing proved a boon for the brewing industry. It enabled draught beer to be served in clear containers rather than pewter ones, while those that could afford the extra expense were able to drink beer at home from bottles in preference to visiting pubs. Glass profoundly boosted the rise of pale ale and bitter. Once drinkers could see what they were drinking, darker milds, porters and stouts went into decline and were replaced by sparkling, clear pale ales.

Change and growth

The final years of the 19th century saw a furious pace of change and growth at the brewery. Twenty-eight pubs were added to the estate in 1895, with 13 of them coming from Pickering's Baldock Brewery. In 1897, Charles bought the substantial Cardington Brewery and pubs. The brewery, close to Bedford, was built around 1862 and owned by Charles

Hickman, who came from a family of butchers. In 1883 Hickman filed for bankruptcy and a year later transferred the business to the Cardington Brewery: in effect Hickman had sold the business to the company. When Charles Wells bought Cardington in June 1897 he displayed a hard-headed and unsentimental side to his nature. The Nottingham Brewery, with a direct train link to Bedford, was also interested in buying some of Cardington's pubs. But Charles bought four Cardington houses in Bedford as well as a store at Rothwell in Northamptonshire – all of which Nottingham was keen to buy – for £5,500. In April 1897 he wrote to Charles Cox, a director of Nottingham Brewery: 'Sorry to stand in your way of getting profit on Bedford & Rothwell purchase. I gave a long price not only to increase my number of houses in Bedford, but to keep other people out and certainly have no intention of selling these licensed houses and stores that I have purchased.' Charles Cox replied phlegmatically: 'I shall be glad to hear when you are getting on with Cardington

COOPERS AND MALTSTERS
POSE WITH THE TOOLS OF
THEIR TRADE AT HORNE
LANE AROUND 1893.

RIGHT, THE CART SHED IN
1910: HORSES WOULD GO
BETWEEN THE SHAFTS TO
DELIVER BEER TO PUBS

Brewery Co and when you take possession.' The Cardington site became a bacon-curing factory, a suitable conversion considering the Hickmans' origins. In Bedford only one of the four pubs bought at the time still survives, the Dewdrop near the hospital. In spite of the purchase of Cardington, loans from Barnard's Bank were repaid by 1898. There were no outstanding loans or overdrafts that year. In 22 years, Charles had increased his personal capital almost six-fold to £120,000.

Charles Wells sailed full steam ahead into the 20th century. More than 26,000 barrels were brewed in 1900, with a profit of close to £15,000. The tied estate stood at 100 pubs and the brewery had no debts. As the owner of the biggest brewing business in the area, Charles could look forward to years of growth and success. In order to meet the demands of pubgoers in the new century, who wanted greater comfort, newly acquired pubs were either extensively renovated or entirely rebuilt. A stone inscribed 'CW' was placed prominently in the facade of every rebuilt house. The following year, beer sales reached a peak of 27,705 barrels. This figure settled down at around 25,000 over the following years. Four of Charles's sons were taken into partnership in 1904: as he had reached the age of 62, he prudently began to plan for the future of the company when he was no longer at the helm.

In 1910 Charles Wells became a private limited company. It was valued at £150,000, with a pub estate of 141. Charles became governing director and controlled just over half the capital. His sons, Ernest, Hayward, Harry and Richard, became directors with equal shares. Richard was also appointed company secretary. Charles insisted that his sons working for the company should live in Bedford, and he firmly vetoed a decision by Richard to live just two miles outside the town following his marriage.

In 1910, when the brewery became a limited company, it was producing XX mild, PA or pale ale, IPA or India Pale Ale, XXX strong ale and SS single stout. Bottled beers were

BREWING WATER IS THE LIFEBLOOD
OF A BREWERY. THE PHOTOS SHOW
THE WATER TOWER AND WELL HEAD
THAT SUPPLIED HORNE LANE

Pale Ale, IPA and Extra Stout. Labelling beers with 'Xs' was a centuries-old tradition dating from the time when monks dominated brewing. They blessed their casks of ale by branding them with Xs: the greater the number of Xs, the stronger the beer. By the 20th century, sales of mild were under challenge from pale ale but it was still the dominant style, favoured by those who worked in heavy manual jobs and who preferred a sweeter beer that restored lost energy. Stout, the strongest version of porter, was popular. Wells brewed two versions, Single and Double: the single version may have been no more than porter by another name. India Pale Ale or IPA was so named as it was first brewed for the colonial trade a century earlier. The Burton brewers, using the

hard spring waters of the Trent Valley, were the most famous producers of IPA but once other brewers learnt how to harden their waters with gypsum and magnesium salts they added IPAs to their portfolios. As the 20th century progressed, pale ale in draught form became better known as Bitter.

One of the most important developments taken by Charles early in the 20th century was a major improvement to the supply of water to the brewery. Water is the lifeblood of any brewery. Even the strongest beer is made up of 90 per cent water, and its mineral composition plays an important role in the flavour and palate of beer. Brewers refer to the water used in the mashing process as 'liquor'. The well on the Horne Lane site supplied water for the maltings, but Charles was anxious to ensure a supply of top quality liquor for the brewing side. In 1902 he had a deep well sunk on the Fitzpatrick Estate at the northern end of Bedford deep in to the rock formation with an excellent water-bearing strata. The town council approved

Charles Wells and his family

RIGHT, THE CHRISTENING OF CHARLES MALTBY WELLS IN SEPTEMBER 1908. BACK ROW, RICHARD WELLS, CHARLES WELLS, JOSEPHINE WELLS AND CHRISTOPHER MALTBY. FRONT ROW, DOROTHY WELLS, MARY MALTBY AND JESSIE MALTBY

JOSEPHINE GRIMBLY, WHO SURVIVED HER HUSBAND CHARLES FOR SOME YEARS. IT WAS HIS LOVE FOR HER THAT ENCOURAGED HIM TO FORSAKE HIS MARINER'S LIFE.

CHARLES WELLS IN HIS POMP AS A LEADING BUSINESSMAN IN BEDFORD.

RIGHT, THE MEMORIAL TO HIM IN THE CEMETERY AT FOSTER HILL ROAD

CHARLES WELLS DIED IN 1914.

HIS FAMILY HOPED FOR A QUIET

FUNERAL BUT THERE WAS A

NOTABLE TURNOUT OF TOWNS

PEOPLE AS THE COFFIN MADE ITS

WAY TO THE CEMETERY CHAPEL

his application for a private water main and agreed to lay the pipes at a cost of five shillings (25 pence) per linear yard. The brewery had to pay the council £25 a year for the water supply. (In 1976, when the new brewery was built, the pipes had to be extended beyond Horne Lane to the new site.) In 1904 Charles sank a new well at his own expense at Franklin's brickfields on Clapham Road. There was considerable scepticism when he claimed that the site had an abundant supply of fresh water that could be used by the town. He was proved right and the council accepted his generous contribution with thanks.

As the First World War loomed on the horizon, the brewery consolidated its business. Only three new pubs were added to the estate during the run-up to 1914, while trade settled down

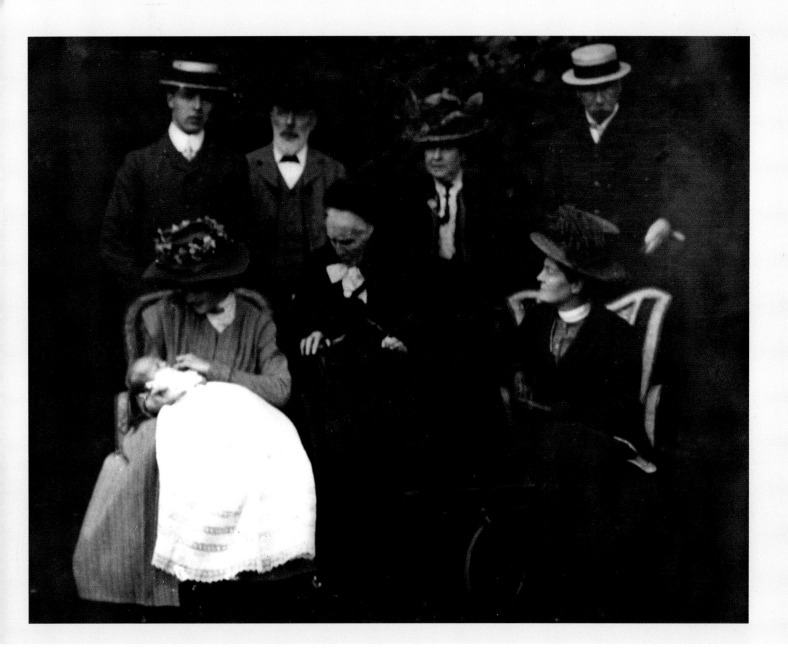

at around 20,000 barrels a year. Profits were healthy and the six-day working week was reduced by closing the brewery on Thursday afternoons.

Charles Wells had been in poor health for several years, with his sons effectively running the company, though he kept his old sailor's hand firmly on the tiller. Charles died on 18 April 1914. He was survived by Josephine, five sons and three daughters. The family hoped for a quiet funeral. This was respected, but there was a notable turnout of Bedford people nonetheless. Charles's coffin had been taken the day before to the cemetery chapel at Foster Hill Road. On the day of the funeral, according to the Bedfordshire Times, 'Shortly before the hour appointed the bells of town churches commenced to toll and a large company of townspeople, tenants and

workpeople had assembled when the mourners arrived'. The sun broke through heavy clouds as the long cortege went from the cemetery church to the graveside, lead by a vicar of St Paul's Church. The funeral arrangements were undertaken by the multi-faceted Wells & Co, who had now added undertaking to their many skills. The newspaper added that Charles Wells would be 'much lamented by the brewery staff, some of whom were old servants. It was a good trait of their employer that he never troubled about their political and religious views'.

Charles Wells was a familiar site in Bedfordshire when he visited his pubs in a pony and trap, or toured the area looking for new sites. He later used a Lanchester car. In the style of Victorian patriarchs and benefactors, he knew all his tenants

by name, and kept a close eye on the fortunes of their families. When Maud Longhurst was born in the Royal Oak at Shefford, Charles gave her mother a shilling. Maud took over the pub and became one of the company's longest-serving tenants. She told a local newspaper, which described her as 'a tiny, rosy-cheeked landlady', that she could remember Mr Wells as 'a real gentleman'. An obituary in the Bedfordshire Times said that he had 'the brusqueness, candour and honesty of the British mariner'.

While he worked long hours at the brewery, he retained his connections with the sea and sailing. He owned a cutter that he kept at Gosport in Hampshire, and he was a member of the Royal Portsmouth Corinthian Yacht Club. He sailed a small boat, the Moorhen, on the River Ouse, and was a member of Bedford Regatta Committee.

Charles was also active in public affairs. He was a County Councillor from 1892 until his retirement in 1907. He served on several committees, including Rate, Finance and General Purposes. He represented East Ward on Bedford Town Council from 1903 until 1909.

He was a generous benefactor at a time when there was no public funding of health care. He also gave financial help to Bedford General Library, and was a supporter of St Paul's Church medical charities and The Nursing Institute. He was a member of the Bedford Board of Guardians and took a keen interest in the plight of boys from impoverished families.

Charles worked prodigiously long hours at the brewery. Thomas Curtis, who went to work at Horne Lane in 1898 straight from school, became a member of the brewing staff. It was his job to check the brewhouse in the evenings and he carried out his duties one Saturday evening in 1910. The next morning Charles Wells called Thomas to his office and said: 'You did not check the brewhouse last night.' 'Yes, I did, sir,' Thomas replied. 'I couldn't hear you,' Charles retorted. 'I was wearing rubber-soled shoes,' Thomas told him. Charles thundered: 'Change them!'

THE IMPRESSIVE FRONTAGE OF
THE WELLS'S SARACEN'S HEAD PUB.
THE CROWNS ON THE ROOF SUGGEST
THE PHOTOGRAPH WAS TAKEN DURING
CELEBRATIONS FOR A CORONATION

The Anchor, Aspley Guise
Michael and Elaine Carpenter

Michael and Elaine Carpenter run a traditional pub, the Anchor at Aspley Guise, where Eagle Bitter is the biggest-selling drink. When they took over the pub, which is more than 100 years old, wine sales were low and they are attempting to build that side of their trade.

Elaine was a hairdresser while Michael ran a sports retail business. Both were keen to get into the pub trade. When they arrived at the Anchor they set about changing its image with new wallpaper and carpets. It needed a brighter atmosphere to appeal to people who wanted to dine. The garden was private but they have changed it into a beer garden with furniture.

The lounge is now used for diners, while a separate bar is for drinkers. Food accounts for 70 per cent of trade. The Carpenters offer steaks, scampi, filled jacket potatoes, curries and children's meals.

Aspley Guise is an affluent village, home to commuters and several millionaires. There's a second pub in the village, also owned by Charles Wells, but it's used mainly by beer drinkers, which gives the Carpenters scope to build their distinctive pub-with-food business. They say they can't afford to stand still in a competitive leisure industry and they have plans to improve the beer garden to attract more customers in the summer.

Turbulent times, steady growth

BREWERS FACED PROFOUND DIFFICULTIES DURING World War One. Managers, employees and experienced publicans were called away on military service, and many never returned. The government placed severe restrictions on the amount of grain breweries could use in order to divert it for bread production. The average strength of beer was reduced drastically as a result. The decline and virtual disappearance of porter during the war was the result of stronger stouts being lowered in strength to the level of porter. David Lloyd George, the Minister of Munitions and a passionate teetotaller, declared that 'Drink is doing us more damage than all the German submarines put together. We are fighting Germany, Austria, and Drink; and as far as I can see the greatest of these deadly foes is Drink'. As a result, licensing hours for pubs were cut in 1914 to brief periods in the middle of the day and the evening, effectively forcing down consumption and production. A year later, using the draconian powers of the Defence of the Realm Act, the government nationalised both breweries and pubs in three areas – most famously Carlisle – with large munitions factories.

Charles Wells was not immune from the impact of the conflict. The family lost Guy Franey Wells, Charles's fifth son, who was killed during the Battle of Ypres in Belgium in 1915.

AMOS WHITE (CENTRE, WEARING APRON), WITH HIS CUSTOMERS OUTSIDE THE THREE TUNS, CASTLE LANE, BEDFORD, IN 1936

A STEAM LORRY BELONGING TO THE NEWPORT PAGNELL
BREWERY. THE COMPANY WAS BOUGHT BY CHARLES WELLS IN
1919. RIGHT, EXAMPLES OF SIMPLE BEER HOUSES OWNED BY
WELLS IN THE EARLY 20TH CENTURY, THE MAGPIE INN AT
HARROLD AND THE BEEHIVE, GREAT BARFORD. BELOW, AN
ADVERTISING CARD FOR WELLS'S MINERAL WATERS

Charles Wells takes to the water

Charles Wells decided in 1915 that it would make mineral waters in addition to beer, to supplement the company's income and to supply its pubs with its own carbonated drinks rather than those of competitors. The directors and shareholders were probably unaware of the stringent demands this simple decision would make from Customs and Excise. Officers were anxious to protect the integrity of beer on which duty was paid. Brewery and mineral factory were strictly segregated, while four windows in a wall dividing the factory and the beer store had to be securely covered with wire gauze to stop any yeast from the brewery section fermenting the sugars in the mineral water. Only loaf sugar or white crystallised sugar were allowed to make mineral water, and the syrup produced had to be flavoured at the time of making. The premises had to be open to inspection by Excise officers at all times.

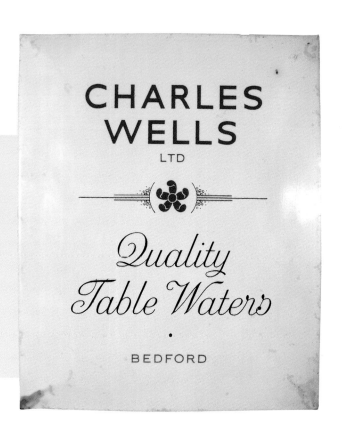

CHARLES
WELLS
LTD

*Quality
Table Waters*

•

BEDFORD

In spite of the restrictions on raw materials, the brewery managed, remarkably, to maintain production at 20,000 barrels a year. Strong beers disappeared for the duration of the war, with production concentrated on a weak mild in which malt was blended with cheaper cereals, colourings and sugar. Pale Ale, Extra Stout and Family Ale, the main bottled brands, were discontinued until the end of the conflict. As well as members of staff, the company also had some of its horses requisitioned for war duty, but by then it was relying more and more on motor vehicles.

Ernest Wells, Charles's oldest son, became chairman on the death of his father. But he and his brother Hayward were away on military service, and the day-to-day running of the business was in the hands of Richard, with the help of Harry. At the annual meeting of the company in 1915, Richard received a vote of thanks for his work and an additional £400 a year while he was in charge.

In May 1917 Richard Wells made a formal offer of £75,000 for the Jarvis Phoenix Brewery in Midland Road. As shown in the second chapter, Walter Jarvis, the owner, had died in 1915 and the business was being run by a receiver and manager, as Jarvis had no children. Wells's offer was later increased to

£90,000. The brewery was taken over in December 1917 and Richard Wells became the manager. The sale was financed by a loan of £60,000 from Parr's Bank, which had taken over Barnard's. Brewing stopped at Midland Road in February 1918. This is traditionally a quiet time in the industry following Christmas and the New Year, and Horne Lane was able to absorb the additional production for the former 66 Jarvis pubs. Richard Wells became the manager of Jarvis to oversee the run-down of the business. Jarvis ceased to exist in May 1920. When Colonel Talbot Jarvis returned from military service he was offered the job of manager of Charles Wells's public house and licensed trade business, which he carried out with considerable flair and success.

Merger plans

Correspondence between the Wells brothers shows that in 1918 they discussed an amalgamation with the two other substantial breweries in Bedford, Newland & Nash and Higgins. The brothers also debated whether to invite the Newport Pagnell Brewery in Buckinghamshire to join the merged group, which would have had an impressive annual output of more than 60,000 barrels. As Horne Lane had the

THE GOLDEN PHEASANT IN BIGGLESWADE:

WELLS MOVED INTO THE AREA WHEN IT

SHARED THE TIED ESTATE OF DAY & CO

WITH WELLS & WINCH OF BIGGLESWADE

best water supply, the other breweries would have closed. The plans came to nothing but the fact that such plans were discussed indicates that Wells was aware that a spate of mergers in the brewing industry in the early 20th century would lead to increased competition. Size, both in terms of brewing capacity and tied estates, was seen as essential to survival as competition grew.

In fact, Wells did not have long to wait to buy the Newport Pagnell Brewery. In July 1919 Charles Wells paid £50,000 to the Allfrey family that owned Newport Pagnell for the share capital. A further £20,000 was raised by an issue of debenture shares to the vendors that paid 5% per annum for five years. An advance of £50,000 was arranged with London Joint City and Midland Bank. Brewing ended at Newport Pagnell during 1919, and brewery and maltings were sold by auction in May

1920. The purchase added 49 freehold and four leased pubs to the Wells's estate. It also gave the Bedford brewery its first steam lorry, a three-ton Foden vehicle. It seems the Wells brothers were not steam enthusiasts as the lorry was sold within the year.

Charles Wells bought further pubs in 1919 when Day & Sons' Priory Brewery in St Neots, Huntingdonshire, was put up for auction. Wells agreed with Wells & Winch of Biggleswade to share the pubs between the two companies. Days's brewery was sold for £40,000 and 27 freehold and three leased pubs were added to the Wells's estate. The Wells brothers were digging deep to expand their business: to cover the cost of the new pubs, a further overdraft of £20,000 was negotiated with London Joint City and Midland Bank. The bank placed a ceiling of £45,000 on the overdraft facility.

The Bedford brewery entered the turbulent 1920s at a furious pace. Activity at the brewery was intense as the production of the Phoenix and Newport Pagnell breweries was absorbed, and the expanded pub estate was supplied with beer and other goods. The commitment of the workforce was recognised in January 1920 when wages for all men working on the site were increased by three shillings (15 pence) a week. In May that year a new pay rate was agreed with the workers' trade union: the maximum weekly rate for men was set between £2 15 shillings (£2.75) and £3 6 shillings (£3.30) a week. Overtime was paid for bank holiday and Sunday working. The workforce became more closely involved in the running of the brewery when a joint committee was set up in 1920 of employees and management. Four hourly-paid workers sat on the committee. Frank Manyweathers, a senior staff member, was secretary, while Hayward Wells represented the directors.

THE BREWERY ENTERED THE

TURBULENT 1920S AT A FURIOUS

PACE, ABSORBING OTHER

BREWERIES AND SUPPLYING

THEIR FORMER PUBS

Dick Harris, from rat catching to hospitality

Dick Harris went to work in the brewery in the 1950s for £3 15s a week. Brewery workers stretched their wages by catching rats, for which they were paid sixpence a time. Rats were a major problem as they were attracted to the grain in the maltings.

Dick recalls one rat that was found dead in the street. It was passed from hand to hand, dusted with grain and even sprayed with paint,

and each time it was presented to a horrified secretary it made the bearer sixpence better off.

He started work at the brewery cleaning tanks and then worked on the bottling line and in the maltings before he was promoted to brewhouse foreman. He left to work elsewhere but returned to Charles Wells, where he became store foreman. He retired eight years ago and worked in total for 45 years at the brewery.

He recalls a time when the brewery was bursting with crates and bottles for light ale, brown ale, barley wine and Guinness. He is full of praise for Roy Morewood: 'He changed the brewery out of all recognition and improved the beer out of all recognition, too.'

Dick now works part-time in the hospitality lounge at the Eagle Centre. His son has worked for Charles Wells for 20 years.

CHARLES WELLS MADE A FURTHER

INVESTMENT IN MUNTON & BAKER

AND FOUR BREWERY DIRECTORS

JOINED THE MUNTON BOARD

Sales in 1920 reached close to 36,000 barrels and the brewery was supplying 290 pubs. Before the absorption of Phoenix and Newport Pagnell, sales had been 21,000 barrels a year, and the number of pubs had totalled 141. Bottled beer production resumed in 1920 after a war-time break and sales rose sharply. As a result, Charles Wells appointed a new head brewer, Stanley Yeo, formerly of Buchan's Breweries of Cardiff. The appointment released his predecessor, Thomas Curtis, to over-see bottled beer production. He spent some time at Young's Brewery in Wandsworth, south London, where he studied at Wickham's bottling plant. He used this experience to improve Wells's bottling line at Bedford.

The death in 1921 of Richard Summers, a director of Newland & Nash, created an opportunity for Charles Wells to buy the brewery, and Hayward and Richard Wells met Claude Clark, who now effectively controlled the Lurke Street company, to discuss a possible merger. Wells's accountants, Beyer, Thomas & Co, were canvassed for their views, but later that year Newland & Nash opened talks with Wells & Winch. A merger was agreed at the end of 1921 and Lurke Street closed in 1924, with production transferred to Biggleswade. As there is no further mention of Newland & Nash in the Charles Wells's minutes, it seems likely that the

board dropped its interest in buying Lurke Street, and decided to concentrate on consolidating its other acquisitions. Charles Wells also had to keep tight rein on its overheads. The loan from the bank was reduced to a maximum of £40,000, but there remained an outstanding payment to the Allfrey family in the form of debenture shares. The Midland Bank agreed to reorganise the financing of the repayment with two debentures of £30,000 that covered all the company's properties. In a further attempt to keep control of expenditure, accountancy procedures were centralised at head office, with all staff employed there and information from subsidiary companies brought under the one roof. A loose-leaf ledger system was introduced. To minimise wastage, the board decided to keep a closer eye on beer quality and brewing efficiency. A monthly report on beer gravities and production losses was set up.

In 1921, Munton & Baker offered £11,500 for the Phoenix Brewery premises. A new company, Munton & Baker (Bedford) Ltd was incorporated in September of that year by the Baker Munton family, with a capital of £15,000. The site was converted to producing malt extract, while the former Phoenix Brewery offices in Midland Road were kept as an off-licence for Charles Wells. Two years, later the capital of Munton & Baker was increased to £25,000. Charles Wells was responsible for the additional capital and the four directors of the brewery joined the board. The name of the company was again changed, this time to Muntona (Bedford) Ltd. The remaining two directors, members of the Baker Munton family, were asked to devote more time to the business and to hold regular monthly board meetings. Malt extract is widely used in baking, confectionery and as a food supplement. It is not used in commercial brewing as it produces a thin beer,

IN THE DAYS BEFORE WINE BECAME POPULAR 'FAMILY' BEERS WERE DESIGNED FOR HOME CONSUMPTION

ridiculed for their ineffectiveness. Hayward Wells had to explain the company's problems to the committee and his reasons were accepted.

The trading difficulties did not prevent the company investing in the brewery. In 1922 two boilers were replaced by one large one, while a shed was built to house a bottling line. The boiler had to be installed with enormous care: it was positioned inside a wall that divided the brewery from a weir in the river. If the river flooded there was a danger the weir might overflow the banks and pour in to the boiler pit. This could have caused a catastrophic explosion, and the siting of the boiler was critical. The range of beers produced at this time was XXX Mild, IPA, and SIPA (Special India Pale Ale) on draught, and FA (Family Ale), FS (Family Stout) and DS (Double Stout) in bottle. The term 'family' was widely

EXAMPLES OF PROMOTIONS BETWEEN THE TWO WORLD WARS FOR WELLS'S BOTTLED BEERS, INCLUDING A STRONG INDIA PALE ALE AND PALE ALE, EXTRA STOUT AND FAMILY ALE

though malt extract is popular with home brewers who do not have the facilities to mash grain.

The brief post-war boom was soon replaced by economic downturn and rising unemployment. Trade suffered as a result and in 1922 the Charles Wells's directors discussed both cutting staff and introducing short-time working. Beer prices to the free trade had to be reduced as a result of increased competition and mineral water prices were also cut. With profit margins falling, employees' wages were reduced by 5s 1d (25p) per week for men and 2s 6d (12.5p) for women and boys. There was considerable anger among the workers over the reductions. The Workers' Committee members were not consulted and complained bitterly that they had been

used at the time, when beer rather than wine was consumed with meals at home.

Josephine Wells remained in Newnham House following the death of her husband. But in July 1924, she decided to vacate the family home and move to Castle Close in Bedford. A substantial part of Newnham House was let to the town council: half the ground floor was kept as offices for the brewery, but the rest of that floor and the two upper storeys were leased to the council. The space was brought back by the brewery in 1960 when it needed to expand its office accommodation.

An indication of the problems that confronted the brewing industry in the early part of the 1920s was seen in Hitchin in Hertfordshire. A slum clearance scheme demolished around 13 pubs in and around the Queen Street area. This gave Charles Wells the opportunity to rebuild the Bricklayers Arms on Queen Street, but trade was slow to build, and six years later, in 1928, the company had to give financial help to the tenant in the form of a rent allowance. As a response to price cutting by other brewers, Charles Wells was forced to reduce its own prices, with Mild sold at 5d (2.5p) a pint. Even so,

Paine's of St Neots and Fullers offered their mild ales at 4d a pint. To add to the company's problems, thieves stole £113.39 in cash plus cheques from a wall safe at the brewery that was used to deposit money overnight prior to being banked. As a result, Edgar Valentine, a brewery traveller, had his journeys rescheduled to avoid his returning to the brewery late at night. The company's two travellers were supplied with cars for added security while pub tenants were encouraged to pay for rent and supplies by cheque.

In the 1920s the brewery moved from horse-drawn to motorised delivery vehicles. In 1922 the directors discussed the fitness of the Old White Horse, which had fallen down in the street while making deliveries. It was decided to keep the horse in service until the end of the year and a vet was asked to kill him humanely if he fell down again, which he did in December. Only four horses remained and were kept strictly for local deliveries. Brewery stables were converted to garages, and the lorry fleet was expanded to eleven. Two motorbikes were kept for use by travellers.

Bottling for the nationals

Small improvements in the economy led to increased beer sales in 1924, with production running at 27,000 barrels for the year. 1924 saw the Starfish trade mark officially registered, while the stores at Rothwell in Northamptonshire, which had been bought from the Cardington Brewery, were sold for £450. The following year, there was an all-time record racking of beer in April, though sales overall for 1925 were slightly down at 26,000 barrels. The bottling department was expanded when the company signed contracts to package Bass and Guinness: it was the custom of the large national brewers to sub-contract the bottling of their products to smaller regional brewers, who had to package supplies of the beers delivered to them in bulk. Wells's own Strong Ale had become a popular bottled brand and was advertised with metal plates on the sides of the company's lorries.

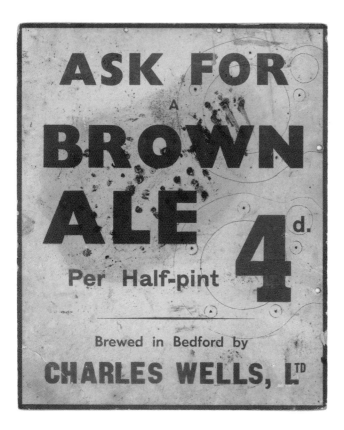

THERE WAS FIERCE
COMPETITION FOR MILD AND
BROWN ALE IN THE 1920S.
WELLS WAS FORCED TO CUT ITS
PRICE TO FOURPENCE FOR A
HALF PINT OF BROWN ALE

BEDFORD DIVISION
PARLIAMENTARY ELECTION.

Thursday, 6th December, 1923.

BEDFORD
v. LUTON.

Play Up, Bedford !

Come in your Thousands,

and

VOTE

for

WELLS,

The Bedford Man.

Printed by the "Bedfordshire Standard" Newspaper Co. (1912), Ltd., 105 High Street, Bedford, and Published by Walter Shepherd, 75 Midland Road, Bedford.

GENERAL ELECTION.

RESULT OF THE POLLS.

Great Bedford Victory.

BEDFORD DIVISION.

Mr. S. R. Wells (C.)	-	12,906
Mr. Milner Gray (Lib.)	-	12,449
Majority	-	457

Mr. S.R. Wells (c) - 12,906
Mr. Milner Gray (Lib) - 12,449
Majority - - 457

[Photo]
The portrait of Mr. S. R. Wells, M.P., as shown on our Election Results Sheet, is by Kingham Studios, Bedford.
IG. A. Gearey.

Richard Wells

Richard Wells became interested in politics
and was an active Conservative. A special
board meeting in January 1922 resolved
that directors could stand for parliament,
with no financial obligations falling on the
company. There was a celebration in
November of that year when Richard was
elected as Conservative Member for
Bedford, with a substantial majority over
three other candidates.

The debenture shares allocated to the Allfrey family following the purchase of the Newport Pagnell Brewery were paid off by the end of 1925. The company was wound up on 5 January 1926, with all properties transferred to Charles Wells. 1926 proved to be a difficult year for the brewing industry and pub trade. A long-running dispute over pay between the miners' trade union and the employers led to the TUC calling out other key unions in support of the pit men. The General Strike in May, which involved more than three million workers, was defeated and all trade unionists, not just the miners, suffered a reduction in wages. The mines dispute led to a shortage of coal for brewers, while general wage cuts reduced demand for beer. In spite of these problems, Wells pressed ahead with modernising several of its pubs, while the directors addressed the problem of a reliable supply of malted barley. The problem had intensified when Wells lost the use of the Ampthill Maltings. The maltings had been rented from Morris & Co, but when Morris was taken over by J W Green of Luton, a regional giant in the area that was subsequently absorbed by Whitbread, the lease was withdrawn.

Boosting malt supply

Wells bought four Morris pubs that Green did not require, and then turned its attention to the supply of malt. £10,000, a substantial sum for the time, was invested in a new malt kiln at Horne Lane. The kiln was in full operation by 1928 and was able to supply not only the brewery's own needs but sold malt on a regular basis to Muntona.

BREWERY TRIPS FOR EMPLOYEES WERE A FEATURE OF THE INTER-WAR YEARS. IN 1920 BUSES WERE HIRED TO TAKE WELLS'S STAFF TO THE DERBY AT EPSOM RACECOURSE

In 1927 the directors agreed that five per cent of the workforce should be disabled ex-servicemen under a government scheme known as the King's Roll. A year later, the company introduced a pension scheme with compulsory retirement at the age of 65 for all employees. Among those that retired that year was head brewer Stanley Yeo. Thomas Curtis, who had been seconded to oversee bottled beer production, was reappointed head brewer and his job was augmented by a consulting brewer and an under brewer, Messrs Chambers and Whitmore. The brewing team was warmly congratulated for winning second prize for Mild Ale at the Brewers' Exhibition. The appointment of a new brewing team underscored a belief held firmly by Charles Wells, the founder, that no member of the family should take on the

Harry Wells

Harry Wells died suddenly in 1925, aged just 47. He suffered a brain haemorrhage. His wife was formerly Amy St Quentin, a leading tennis player. Harry was an enthusiastic tennis player, too, and he also collected stamps, did carpentry – he built the present boardroom table – and was a keen photographer. He took photos of most of the company's pubs, travelling round the estate in his Model T Ford car. The Bedfordshire Times paid tribute to this gregarious local character who had been educated at Bedford School. He went to France in 1915 with a motor ambulance and was later commissioned in the Royal Army Service Corps.

post of head brewer. His view was that it could create awkward situations if a batch of beer was unsatisfactory and led to complaints from customers. The policy has been retained to the present day.

The company further eased its problems with the supply of malt in 1928 when Higgins & Sons' Castle Brewery was sold to Wells & Winch. Production ceased in October 1928. The premises were sold off piecemeal in 1929 and Charles Wells bought the brewery maltings, together with offices and a bottle-washing shed for £1,100. Josephine Wells was renting the former manager's house, with a substantial garden and greenhouse, and this was also purchased for £750. The additional maltings capacity was quickly absorbed by Wells, and it was able to meet an order for 4,000 quarters of malt from Muntona. Demand for both bottled beer and soft drinks led to both new bottling plant, and filling and syruping machines being installed. The age of the horse finally disappeared when the last horse-drawn van was replaced by a new 30cwt Ford lorry and the remaining stable was converted to a garage. By the end of the decade, the brewery had an eleven-strong fleet of vehicles.

Charles Wells won another second-place prize in the 1928

ECONOMIC PROBLEMS IN THE 1930S DID NOT STOP THE DIRECTORS FROM ADDING NEW VESSELS

Brewers' Exhibition, this time for bottled Light Bitter. The range of beers being brewed at the time included SIPA, XXX mild, IPA and Double Stout in cask, with FA (Family Ale), SA (Strong Ale), and FS (Family Stout) in bottle.

The company entered the 1930s with sales of beer registering 28,000 barrels. This figure was substantially down on sales a decade earlier, an indication of the problems caused by heavy unemployment and depressed wages. But the confidence of the directors can be seen in the decision to add four new slate fermenting vessels. Slate at the time was a much-favoured material for fermenters as it was thought that it reacted with beer to create a natural carbonation and lively head of foam. The roof of the copper house was renewed, the bottling plant was extended yet again, and six 20-barrel

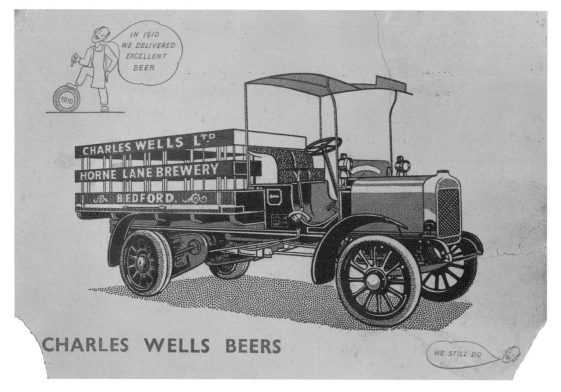

AN EARLY 20TH-CENTURY EXAMPLE OF A MOTORISED DRAY USED TO DELIVER CHARLES WELLS'S BEER

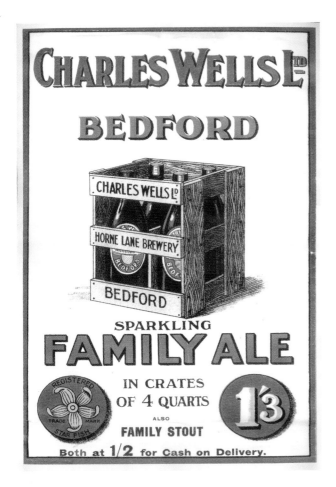

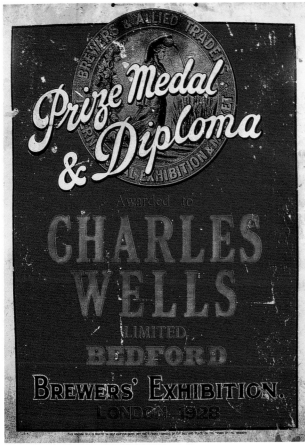

conditioning tanks were installed. The company's capital was increased in 1930 from £150,000 to £270,000, divided equally between ordinary and preference shares: this was achieved with a distribution to family shareholders from a reserve fund along with undistributed profits. There was a further award from the Brewers' Exhibition of a silver medal for draught Family Ale.

By 1931 production had settled down to around 27,000 barrels a year. The problems of the economy forced the directors to be prudent. They were careful not to take too much from profits and, with all outstanding loans repaid, were able to place £20,000 on deposit with the Midland Bank and buy £20,000-worth of war loan bonds. A new pasteurisation plant for bottled beer was installed along with four more conditioning tanks. Bottled beers at the time were Pale Ale, Family Ale, Family Stout, Double Stout and Strong Ale. The company again scored well in the Brewers' Exhibition, winning two third prizes for bottled Strong Ale and draught Mild Ale. The company took legal action against Jordan & Addington of St Neots and other soft drink manufacturers to stop them selling their products in Wells's public houses: a court injunction was published in the local press.

Two of the sons of Richard Wells joined the brewery in 1931. Charles Maltby Wells, Richard's eldest son, had an engineering degree and had worked in a large Canadian engineering company. He joined the family brewery to help with outside management and accountancy. James Maltby Wells, Richard's third son, came to the brewery to learn about grain, malt and bottling. But James's first love was flying and he later left the brewery for a full-time job in aviation. He also became a member of an RAF auxiliary squadron.

Hayward Wells replaced his brother Ernest as chairman of the company. Richard Wells had become a prominent local figure and the Bedfordshire Times reported an 'enthusiastic gathering' at Bedford Corn Exchange on 7 October 1932 when Richard and his wife Dorothy were presented with gifts

THE BREWERY PROMOTED ITS

FAMILY ALE AND ITS

BREWERS'S EXHIBITION

AWARDS DURING THE 1920S

The soul of beer

The reason for Charles Wells's insatiable need for malt in the 1930s was a simple one: barley malt is the essential raw ingredient used in the brewing process. Brewers call malt 'the soul of beer'. Other grain – wheat, maize, oats, rye and rice – can be used to make beer, but barley is the preferred grain because it is rich in the starch that is converted to fermentable sugar; it gives a delightful juicy and biscuity flavour to beer; and it has a husk that acts as a natural filter during the initial mashing stage in the brewery.

England produces some of the finest malting barley in the world. Norfolk, known as the country's 'grain basket', is the main source of barley, which flourishes in the rich, dark soil. Most barley goes for cattle feed, nourishing drinks such as Ovaltine and Bournvita, and is used in confectionery. Only the finest barley, low in nitrogen, can be used to make ales. When the grain is harvested it is taken to a maltings where it is thoroughly washed or 'steeped' in water to start the growing process. In a traditional floor maltings, the grain is spread on large, heated floors and forms what is called a piece. The grain is turned by hand with wooden shovels to aerate it, and to prevent the shoots interlocking. In a drum maltings, the grain is turned as the drum revolves. The warm air encourages the grain to germinate: the starch in the grain becomes soluble, which enables it to be transformed into fermentable sugar during the brewing process. The clear sign that germination is taking place is the rootlet breaking through the husk.

Hidden from view, the plant's embryo – the main root or acrospire – starts to grow, triggering a change that turns proteins into enzymes. The enzymes will convert starch to sugar in the mash tun in the brewery. Only partial germination takes place: if the grain was allowed to fully germinate, it would start to consume its own vital sugars. The skill of the maltster is to judge when partial germination has gone far enough. He does this by the age-old device of chewing some: if the grain is soft and 'friable' in the mouth, then modification –

the growth of the embryo and the solubility of the starch – has progressed successfully.

The grain is transferred to a kiln where it is spread on slotted floors. Heat from gas fires comes blasting up from below and dries the wet or 'green' malt. Brewers want predominantly pale malt, the result of a relatively short kilning or curing. This preserves the high level of enzymes in the malt that will convert starch to sugar. Darker malts, such as amber, brown, black and chocolate, are heated

HOPS ARE FAMOUS FOR

ADDING BITTERNESS TO

BEER BUT ALSO GIVE HERBAL

AND SPICY AROMAS

to a higher temperature. Heavily roasted malts, such as black and chocolate, are used for colour and flavour in stout and other dark beers. Many British brewers add some specialist malt called crystal to their bitters. This is the case with both Charles Wells's Eagle and Bombardier. Crystal is a 'stewed' malt. After partial germination, the grain is placed in a sealed drum so the moisture cannot escape. The temperature is raised to 45 degrees C, which matches the mashing temperature in a brewery. The enzymes inside each kernel of grain convert some of the starches to sugar. The temperature is then raised so that the sugar crystallises (toffee is made in a similar fashion). The grain is added to the pale malt in the mash tun and adds a fullness of palate and slight sweetness to the finished beer.

Hops are famous for adding bitterness to beer. But the remarkable small, green climbing plant – a relation of both the common nettle and cannabis – does far more than that. It also

A FIELD OF BARLEY GROWING IN THE
'GRAIN BASKET' OF BRITAIN. ONLY THE FINEST,
LOW-NITROGEN BARLEY CAN BE USED IN
BEER MAKING. ABOVE, A MALTSTER CHECKS
THE FINISHED GRAIN MADE IN A MODERN
DRUM MALTINGS

gives aromas and flavours to beer that, depending on the variety used, may be spicy, peppery, herbal, resiny, perfumy and citrussy. The hop gives added dimensions and depth to beer and balances the sweetness of the malt. Hops, grown in Kent, Herefordshire and Worcestershire, are picked in the early autumn, and dried and packed into giant sacks called pockets. Some brewers prefer to use the whole hop flower, others use compressed hop pellets or extracted oils. In the brewery, hops are added in a boiling copper to the sweet extract known as wort. Hops and wort are boiled vigorously for an hour or more, during which time the resins and oils from the hops are absorbed into the liquid.

The hops are usually added at several stages during the boil, as some of the aroma and flavour are distilled into the atmosphere: brewers call this 'the angels' share'. The hop oils, resins and natural acids also act as a preservative, keeping infection out of beer. Lager brewers use hops with less aggressive aromas and flavours than English ale varieties. The finest lager hops are grown in southern Germany and the Czech Republic.

Even the strongest beer is made up of 90% water, and the quality of water is vital to the brewing process. Some breweries have their own natural wells on site, others use the public supply. In either case, the water – known as 'liquor' in a brewery – will be thoroughly cleaned and filtered. Ale brewers need hard water and will often add such salts as gypsum and magnesium to their liquor. This is known as 'Burtonisation', as it replicates the hard waters of Burton-on-Trent in the English Midlands, where pale ale was first successfully brewed in the 19th century. Lager brewers, on the other hand, prefer soft water that brings out the silky smoothness of their beers.

Beer cannot be made without yeast. Yeast is a type of fungus that converts malt sugars into alcohol during the fermentation process. Each brewery jealously guards its yeast culture and stores it in cool, refrigerated conditions. Yeast not only produces alcohol but also adds flavour to beer: the house yeast of a particular brewery is its taste signature. There are two types of yeast: ale yeast, which is called warm or top fermenting; and lager yeast, known as cold or bottom fermenting. During fermentation, ale yeast rises to the top of the liquid and creates a thick blanket or head. Lager yeast works more slowly at colder temperatures and continues to convert remaining sugars into alcohol during the second stage of fermentation known as cold maturation: the German word is 'lager', meaning storage. In many modern breweries, such as Charles Wells, where all beers – ale and lager – are fermented in conical vessels, the difference between the two types of yeast is now minimal.

Ernest Wells

Tragedy struck the brewery when Ernest Wells, the eldest son of Charles, and chairman since 1914, died suddenly from pneumonia on 11 September in 1932 while he was on holiday with his family at Frinton-on-Sea in Essex. Ernest had lived at Turvey Abbey for the past nine years. When he left school, he was articled to Robey Engineers of Lincoln. While he was in Lincoln, he badly injured one of his legs in a shooting accident. He never allowed his disability to affect his work or leisure. He went to work for the family brewery and became interested in athletics. He was also a keen tennis player. He was given a commission in the Bedford Volunteers and served in both the Boer War and World War One. He was a former High Sheriff for Bedfordshire and was actively involved in many local charities.

to mark both their twenty-fifth wedding anniversary and Richard's ten years as a Member of Parliament. He had fought and won five elections. More than 2,000 people contributed money for the gifts and a total of £102 was collected.

When Charles Maltby Wells was appointed as a director on the first day of January 1934, trade had risen to almost 30,000 barrels a year. The company used the new technology of the day to promote its beer, with screen advertisements in fifteen cinemas in and around Bedford, while a riverside neon sign was erected on one side of the brewery. The pub estate numbered 259, down from a peak of 290 in 1920. Uneconomic pubs had closed, others had been built or bought, and many had been modernised to provide the type of facilities expected by a more discerning clientele. Inside flushing lavatories had become standard in Wells's pubs in and around Bedford.

When Charles Wells had started his business in the 19th century, Bedford had many small, competing breweries. The year 1935 marked an historic moment: Charles Wells became the only brewer left in the town. In January it bought Fuller's Brewery in Lurke Street for £12,500, which included the premises and three pubs. The site was sold to Bedford Land Company for £2,500 and became an extension to the Granada cinema car park. The Fuller's brass plate was relocated to the Horne Lane Brewery.

BEER LABELS WERE USED TO PROMOTE WELLS'S BOTTLED ALES WHILE (ABOVE RIGHT) PUB ASHTRAYS ADVERTISED THE COMPANY'S LEMONADE. DID THE MINERAL WATER EASE SMOKER'S COUGH?

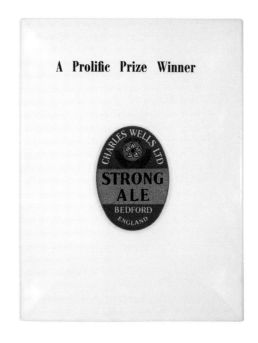

A Prolific Prize Winner

Plans to produce malt in a modern and more effective manner sparked a dispute among the directors. Space was found at the Horne Lane site in 1935 to install a new pneumatic drum maltings with a capacity of 5,000 quarters of grain. The drum maltings was designed by the leading supplier of malting equipment, Robert Boby & Sons of Bury St Edmunds.

Move to modern malting

The plan was to replace the traditional, labour-intensive method of spreading malt on a large floor – where it was turned by hand while it germinated – by four steel drums in which the grain was turned mechanically as the drums revolved. Air circulated under pressure through ducts on the sides of the drums. After four days, when partial germination was complete, the grain would be transferred to a kiln for drying and curing, when it became malt. The Boby malting would have released the floor maltings area, which could have stored wine, spirits and bottled beer. Chairman Hayward Wells and his fellow directors had several disagreements about the new maltings, to such an extent that the plans had to be shelved. In October 1937, the board instructed Hayward to take a complete rest from his duties. He was given six months'

leave to visit Australia and New Zealand. Charles Ian Ballantine Wells, son of the late Charles Ernest Wells, was appointed as a director. Given the brewery's urgent need for malt, malting capacity at Lurke Street was increased and the Castle maltings was bought for £3,500.

The Boby drum maltings was finally commissioned and installed as the decade was drawing to an end with another world war looming.

The company ended the 1930s in good heart despite the prospect of war. Charles Wells was producing 34,000 barrels of beer a year and owned 265 pubs in Bedfordshire, Buckinghamshire, Cambridgeshire, Hertfordshire, Huntingdonshire and Northamptonshire. All the pubs were within a thirty-mile radius of the brewery and were supplied by fourteen delivery lorries. But the outbreak of hostilities with Germany in September 1939 brought immediate changes. The planned alterations to two pubs were postponed. A war wage increase of two shillings (5p) was brought in for male workers, with one shilling for women. The brewery supplied bottled beer to the NAAFI (Navy, Army and Air Force Institute), while a three-ton Commer lorry was requisitioned by the army for military use.

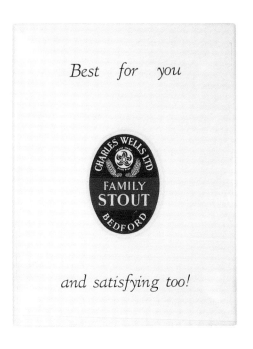

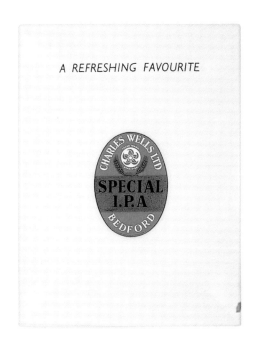

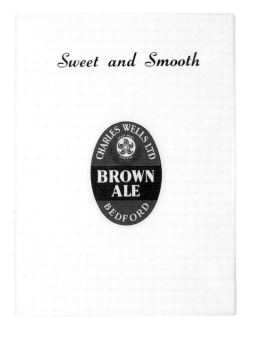

Devonshire Arms, Bedford
Valerie Walter

Valerie Walter knows Charles Wells from both sides of the bar. She worked at Horne Lane and Havelock Street for 25 years, and is best remembered as John Wells's Personal Assistant. Since leaving the brewery in 1998, she has been the licensee of the Devonshire Arms in Dudley Street in Bedford, where she has built a reputation as a publican who serves a good pint and has a brilliant knowledge of quality wines.

Valerie went to work at Horne Lane in 1974 where her main job was to produce circulars for both the tied and free trade. 'I typed the circulars on "skins" that were clamped on to Gestetner office printing machines,' she recalled. 'I had a team of office girls who would stuff the circulars into envelopes with the aid of a drop of beer that had been left by the directors.'

There were no departmental distinctions at Horne Lane. 'The tied and free trades, as well as marketing, were all under one roof, and I also acted as the front office or reception'. At the same time, Valerie was gaining experience of pub life by working in the evenings in a Bedford pub called the Falstaff, owned at the time by Bass Charrington. She was devastated when John Wells told her he was retiring from the board in January 1998. She was offered another job in the brewery but she decided to run a pub with a friend and they were lucky to discover that the licensee of the Devonshire Arms had given his notice.

Valerie has energetically built the trade of the pub in a residential area. She doesn't open lunchtimes during the week, as there isn't sufficient business, but she is busy in the evenings and weekends. The pub is a popular location for wedding receptions and other events. As well as Eagle and Bombardier, Valerie serves Old Speckled Hen as a guest beer, and once a year she stages a renowned beer festival.

But her main claim to fame is her knowledge and enthusiasm for wine that have won her the Wine Pub of the Year award. She takes great pride in serving wines in the correct glasses, which she has specially imported from Germany, and has twenty wines on offer on a chalk board in the pub.

An era of change and challenge

THE SECOND WORLD WAR, in common with the first, left its mark on the brewery. Three sons of Sir Richard and Lady Wells were killed in action. Squadron Leader James Michael Wells died while flying over the Netherlands in May 1940. He was a skilled pilot. In 1938 the entertainer George Formby starred in the film It's In the Air that featured some acrobatic flying. James Wells performed the stunts though Formby appeared to be at the controls. Just one month after James died, Lt-Commander Christopher Hayward Wells went down with the aircraft carrier HMS Glorious, which was sunk during the Norwegian campaign against the Germans. There were further blows in 1942. Major Thomas Capper Wells, a son of Sir Richard Wells, was serving with the Bedfordshire and Hertfordshire Regiment in Singapore when the Japanese invaded and he was killed in action. Charles Ian Wells, son of Ernest, was on duty with the Royal Artillery when he was killed in an accident during military manoeuvres. He had served in France and returned to England during the Dunkirk evacuation. At the start of the war, Major Charles Wells and Captain Ian Wells were put on half salary while they served in the army.

On the home front, the brewery escaped largely unscathed from a war that saw saturation bombing of London and other major cities, ports and docks. The most dramatic event at Horne Lane was the collapse of part of the brewery wall that fell into the river in 1944 and which had to be repaired urgently at a cost of £2,000. Only crucial repairs to buildings were permitted, but the brewery chimney was considered essential work and renovation was carried out. Air raid shelters were installed at the bottom of the concrete maltings so that employees could seek safety in the event of an air raid. As a result of orders from the Home Office, wages for both brewery and maltings workers were increased: records show that in 1940 maltings workers were paid a total of £4 a week for 56 hours.

The company experimented with managed public houses, a break from the tradition of tied houses run by self-employed tenants. Six pubs were switched to salaried managers, which allowed the company to retain the retail profits of some of its bigger pubs. The management scheme was eventually expanded to some thirty pubs. The scheme enabled the brewery to control the standards of each pub and the price of beer in public bars as an example of good value for customers.

Wartime delivery

The war did not affect production or consumption of beer. 40,000 barrels were produced in 1941. In order to save fuel, Charles Wells entered into an agreement with other brewers to deliver beer to pubs outside immediate delivery areas. Dale & Co, for example, took Wells's beer to the Ancient Druids and Wrestlers in Cambridge. Fordham of Ashwell delivered to Hitchin and Stotfold for Wells, while Wells supplied

A MORE MODERN IMAGE FOR WELLS'S ADVERTISING IN POST-WAR BRITAIN (RIGHT). NOGGIN (ABOVE) WAS THE BREWERY'S RESPONSE TO THE 'KEG REVOLUTION'

WELLS ALES ARE WONDERFUL

BY CHARLES WELLS OF BEDFORD OF COURSE

Fordham's pubs in Clophill and Sharnbrook. The formal arrangement lasted for only a few months but Dale agreed to continue to deliver to two Wells's pubs in the Fenstanton area.

Strict rationing made an impact on all parts of the brewery. Only four beers were brewed for the duration of the war in order to preserve supplies of malt and hops. XX Mild and SIPA were available on draught while the bottled beers were pale ale and stout. From 1942 bottle deposits were invoiced separately to customers: with a shortage of bottles it was essential to keep track of empties. Casks were also in short supply and draymen were given special allowances for collecting empty containers from pubs.

The contentious new drum maltings was finally built and started to operate early in the war. Wells had to supply Muntona as well as its own needs and was suffering from a severe shortage of labour as a result of the military call-up. Arthur Guinness arranged for six maltsters to travel from Ireland to work in the Wells's maltings. It is not recorded whether the Irish government, which was neutral during the war, approved of Guinness's help for Wells, but the Dublin company did not act out of pure altruism as it needed supplies of malt from Wells for its London brewery at Park Royal. With the drum maltings in operation, Wells closed the Castle Maltings and the buildings were sold to the town council.

1945 was a memorable year. It marked the end of the war, deaths abroad, and deprivation and hardship at home. Wells brewed a remarkable volume of 47,000 barrels to help celebrate victory. Employees who worked during a special week of national celebrations were rewarded with an additional week's pay and those who worked on VE (Victory

Oliver Wells

Oliver Wells, the youngest son of Sir Richard, was appointed Executive Director in May 1956. He was a war hero, a bomber pilot who was shot down while flying a Lancaster. He was picked up by the French Resistance and almost made it safely back to Britain. But he was caught by the Germans and became a prisoner of war. His camp was liberated by the Russian Red Army and he returned to active duty, making many hazardous flights during the Berlin Airlift.

in Europe) Day were given double pay plus two days' holiday.

There were some notable exits and entrances as peace returned to war-shattered Britain. George Cotton retired as chief clerk: he had started work in the industry with Jarvis's Phoenix Brewery in 1910. Frank Manyweathers, head of the office, had an even more impressive record. He retired in 1946, having started with Charles Wells in 1886 at the age of fourteen. Major David Wells MC, son of Sir Richard, joined the brewery to manage the tied estate with Talbot Jarvis. Jarvis retired soon after. Major Wells was a career soldier who had joined the Royal Artillery in 1933, and won his Military Cross during the Burma campaign. He was reluctant to leave the army but was persuaded to join the family business. Squadron Leader Pat Wells DSO, the son of Eric, also joined the brewery. He had fought gallantly during the Battle of Britain and

suffered severe burns when his Hurricane fighter was shot down on November 28, 1940.

The most significant development of the late 1940s and 1950s was a consumer switch to bottled beer. One argument advanced for this change in drinkers' tastes was that many experienced publicans had been killed during the war – either as a result of military service or bombing during the Blitz – and their replacements had little experience in cellaring and serving cask-conditioned beer. Filtered and star-bright bottled beers were demanded by drinkers tired of being served cloudy and poorly conditioned draught ale. Charles Wells, in common with all brewers with adequate resources, had to meet the demand by installing new bottling machines. In 1947 a considerable amount of work was carried to the brewery's cool, refrigeration and fermenting rooms, while the bottled beer and mineral water plants were rebuilt, requiring 25 tons of steel girders. Bottles were given a stronger brand image with labels incorporating the Starfish trade mark. The importance of the bottled beer market was underscored by a decision to order a new diesel generator as a standby for the bottling department in case of power cuts, which were a feature of the immediate post-war years as a result of bitterly cold winters and a shortage of coal. The brewery's boilers were converted to oil to avoid too much reliance on coal.

Draymen's grievances

In 1947, when the government's annual Budget increased the duty on beer, Charles Wells was producing X Mild at 11d a pint, SIPA, Pale Ale and Family Stout (1s 3d each). A Strong Ale in bottle was introduced at 1s 1d.

A threatened strike by draymen that year was called off following a meeting with David Wells, who was able to sort out their grievances. David had taken up an executive role with the company, while Aileen Wells, the daughter of Ernest, was appointed a non-executive director: she was one of the first women to be given a leading role in the industry. In that year, Pat Wells left to take up a career in South Africa, where he

VICTORY CELEBRATIONS TO MARK THE
END OF THE WAR. THE HAPPY PEOPLE OF
KIRKMAN CLOSE, BEDFORD, NO DOUBT
ENJOYED SOME CHARLES WELLS'S BEERS

had been brought up, while Charles Maltby Wells, the elder grandson of the founder, moved to Canada to work for Canada Maltings.

Production of bottled Brown Ale resumed in 1947 and two years later a new and stronger XX Mild was introduced. Unusually, XX Mild was launched in conjunction with a similar beer brewed by Wells & Winch, and both beers were jointly advertised.

Horace Munton Baker MBE, the chairman of Muntona, died in a London nursing home in December 1949. Sir Richard Wells was appointed chairman of Muntona, which was still operating on the site of the former Phoenix Brewery. Malt extract was a successful product and Muntona was keen to have greater and independent control over the supply of grain. A redundant factory in Stowmarket in Suffolk, in the heart of the East Anglian grain belt, was bought with help from Charles Wells.

A major change in Charles Wells's boardroom structure took place in 1950 when Thomas Curtis was appointed a director in recognition of his long and valuable service to the brewery. He was the first director to come from outside the family, and his appointment required a change to the company's articles of association. In the new social climate of post-war Britain, the Wells family recognised the need to draw talent from a wider circle. Curtis left school at the age of thirteen and started work at the brewery as an office boy. He became interested in brewing and was taught the skills by the then head brewer, George Cocking. Curtis fought in the First World War, returned to the company and became head brewer in 1928.

Thomas Curtis joined the board at a difficult time for family brewers. Such large regional groups as Bass Worthington, Ind Coope, Watney and Whitbread, as well as the Anglo-Irish giant Guinness, were forging ahead with bottled beer sales as a result of their ability to advertise nationally. Bottled Double

THE BREWERY FACED A NEW

CHALLENGE AS THE NATIONALS

FORGED AHEAD WITH HEAVILY

PROMOTED BOTTLED BRANDS

Diamond and Guinness became cult brands, and smaller firms found trading difficult. Charles Well recorded a serious fall in trade and, as a result, property repairs and alterations had to be scaled down. On a more positive note, the brewery won a first prize for Strong Ale and second prize for stout at the Brewers' Exhibition. The BBC Light Programme's Music While You Work was piped to workers in the new bottled beer stores, a sign of how important packaged beer was to the company and the need to keep the workforce content. Strong Ale was supported with 1,500 showcards, while the Starfish trade mark was registered for a further fourteen years. Customers' needs were also kept in mind: the Harpur Arms in Bedford was the first pub in the estate to have air conditioning installed.

Full range

In 1952, Sir Richard Wells MP, the last surviving son of the founder, became chairman. He was joined by two new directors from outside the family, Edmund Stansfield and Horace Tebbs. The directors pursued a policy of converting beer houses – pubs licensed to sell beer only – to full on-licensed premises that offered a full range of drinks. Customers were demanding better amenities in pubs, but the brewery faced a backlog of repairs and renovations. They were difficult to carry out as the government placed restrictions on building work that was not considered essential: priority was given to repairing war-damaged homes. Charles Wells decided to build new pubs wherever possible. The Turnpike at Eascotts and the Sportsman at Goldington, both on the outskirts of Bedford, were built but were restricted in size as a result of government regulations.

1953 was Coronation Year and a bottled Coronation Ale was brewed and sold for 1s 6d a half pint. All 136 employees were presented with a 5s (25p) souvenir Coronation coin. A new draught Light Bitter was introduced and sold for 1s 1d. Special IPA replaced bottled Light Ale. The malting side of the business increased steadily, with contract work for Hugh Baird and Guinness, and it was necessary to buy a Bedford tractor unit with a 10-ton Scammell trailer to transport bulk grain. The directors pushed ahead with upgrading public houses, most of which were by now fully licensed.

A sign of the times – and the future – was marked in 1954 when Charles Wells began to supply bottled Barclays Lager to

Hayward Wells

Colonel Hayward Wells died in June 1952 at his home, Ickwell Bury. He was educated at Bedford School, became a governor of the Harpur Trust, and a benefactor to both schools. He was a town councillor in the 1920s and became Mayor of Bedford in 1931-2. He was a keen oarsman and helped organise the Bedford Regatta. As well as his duties as a director of the brewery, he also had a working knowledge of brewing. In World War One he commanded a division of the Royal Engineers at Gallipoli and later fought in Egypt. He bought the site of Ickwell Bury in 1937 after the house had burned down and had it rebuilt by 1940. He nominated his wife, Mary, to be a member of the board of Charles Wells. He left Ickwell Bury for the use of Bedford School.

THE DEMAND FOR BOTTLED BEER IN POST-WAR BRITAIN CAN BE
SEEN IN THIS DELIVERY BY ROLY COOK (LEFT) AND ALBERT PHELAN
TO A WELLS'S PUB, WITH CRATES OUTNUMBERING CASKS

its pubs. But at the same time, sales of its own beer were at last beginning to show an increase. From a low of 23,000 barrels that year, production increased to 26,000 barrels in 1955 and rose to 27,000 by 1956. In 1955 three pubs were purchased from the Bedford Estate while the demand for malt made it necessary for Wells to employ maltsters for the whole year, rather than seasonally. The draught beers produced at this time were XX Mild, IPA and SIPA, while the bottled beers were Pale and Brown Ale, Family Stout and Strong Ale. Contract bottling was done for Barclays, Bass, Guinness and Worthington.

An era ended in December 1956 with the death of Sir Richard Wells, one of the most remarkable servants the brewery had known. He was an original director in 1910 and chairman from 1952. He also served as chairman of Muntona and its associate company, Edward Fison Ltd. He was a member of the council of the Brewers' Society for forty years and the society's chairman from 1940 to 1942. He was only the second holder of a driving licence in Bedfordshire, dating from 1904. He married Dorothy Maltby in 1907 and her maiden name was enshrined in the forenames of younger members of the Wells family. Richard and Dorothy had seven sons and two daughters. He was a county councillor and Conservative MP for Bedford from 1922 to 1945. He was knighted in 1937 and created a baronet in 1944.

Richard and Dorothy knew great sadness: three of their sons – Christopher, James and Tom – were killed in World War Two. At their silver wedding party in 1932, Dorothy Wells recalled her first attempt at electioneering for Richard at a local factory. The Bedfordshire Times reported that 'she undertook the task with trembling limbs and faltering voice'. At the end of her short speech, she blurted out a few unscripted words: 'My husband is the best and straightest man I have ever known'. A man in the crowd turned to Richard and said, 'That's a feather in your cap, guv'nor'. A New Year message sent to Richard by Horace Baker Munton in January 1939 was preserved in Richard's scrapbook:

Said the PM to our Gracious King
In Bedfordshire there dwells
A man whose praises I can sing
By name, S. Richard Wells.
His country he has served all right
With gumption and goodwill.
I suggest that he be made a KNIGHT
It tis your Royal Will.

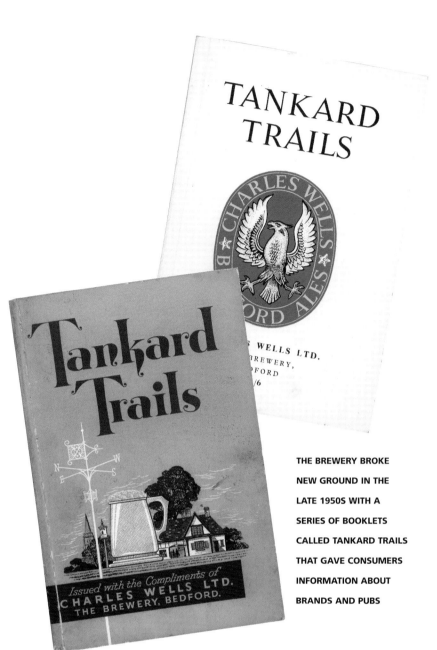

THE BREWERY BROKE NEW GROUND IN THE LATE 1950S WITH A SERIES OF BOOKLETS CALLED TANKARD TRAILS THAT GAVE CONSUMERS INFORMATION ABOUT BRANDS AND PUBS

David Wells was appointed chairman and managing director at the 1957 annual general meeting. A year later, Oliver became joint managing director. Sir Richard Wells had left a powerful legacy with two of his sons at the helm, brothers who were also grandsons of the founder, Charles Wells. They set about quietly but firmly refashioning the business to meet the changing needs of the time. With major bottled beer brands rampant, smaller brands needed names that chimed with the times. Old Bedford Ale was introduced for the winter trade while Strong Ale in bottle was rebranded Fargo Strong Ale, a name that would come back to haunt the company in later years. Fargo was advertised on ten bus sides and the beer was further boosted by an order for 3,000 bottle openers that carried its name.

Muntona ended its long association with Bedford in 1959 when it opened a new plant in Stowmarket and concentrated production of malt extract there. The company was restructured as Munton and Fison, and it vacated the former Jarvis Brewery site in Bedford, which Charles Wells bought back. New pubs were added to the estate in Allhallows, Dunstable, Great Brickhill and Hitchin.

The national brewers were spending large amounts on advertising, and Charles Wells, in a humbler manner, had to follow suit to keep its beers in the public eye. In 1959, the board agreed an annual advertising budget of £3,000. The following year, the brewery also sanctioned the publication of a company handbook by the specialist publishers Ed Burrows. It was the first of a series of booklets called Tankard Trails that, at a time when most brewers were reluctant to disclose information about their activities, gave details about the brewery, with a list of all the company's pubs, which now numbered 293. At the same time, a new sign announcing CHARLES WELLS LTD BEDFORD BREWERY was erected at the brewery to stress its central role in the town.

The 'Swinging Sixties' were to see many changes in brewing practice and beer styles. There was an early sign of the times in 1960 when Wells introduced Flowers Keg Bitter to the Southend Hotel in Bedford. It was the first of several Wells's pubs that took the processed beer in the early years of the decade. Keg beer was not the only innovation. Mergers among brewers were to change the face of the industry and put independent regional producers under enormous pressure. In 1960 Jack Redman of Wells & Winch held informal talks with David Wells about a merger. The idea was gently turned down. A merger would have meant Charles Wells losing its family control and becoming a public company. Redman also had talks with McMullen of Hertford and Greene King of Bury St Edmunds. The result was a merger of Greene King and Wells & Winch in 1961. Greene King already owned Simpsons Brewery of Baldock and it now enjoyed a greater presence in East Anglia and the northern Home Counties.

The emergence of Greene King as a major regional brewer did no harm to Charles Wells, which was enjoying a boom in sales. A new bottling line and fermenting room were opened. The brewery went on to a five-day, 42-hour working week to cope with demand as production rose to 32,000 barrels. Further improvements were made to the brewing plant, including bulk silos for malt handling. Peter Steer Jones was appointed assistant brewer and Ray Shreeves was appointed bottling manager at a time when the company's share capital was increased to 350,000 ordinary shares of £1 each, and 100,000 preference shares also worth £1 each. Another sign of changing times and consumer demand came with the setting up of the Jarvis Wine Company to operate retail shops and make wine as well as beer and spirits available to customers.

The Bird In Hand, Brickhill Drive, Bedford, was added to an estate that was now supplied with two keg beers, Draught Guinness and Flowers. It was the success of Flowers Keg Bitter that prompted a merger of ground-shaking importance in 1961. J W Green of Luton was a great presence in Bedfordshire and Hertfordshire, and was one of the biggest and most successful regional brewers in Britain. It had become a public company in the 1930s and merged with Flowers of Stratford upon Avon in 1954. The company was driven by Bernard Dixon, who started with Greens as a brewer but rose to become managing director. His uncompromising approach to business did not win many friends but he was immensely successful and influential. He was determined to turn Greens into a national company and saw keg beer as the way to achieve his ambition. To this end, he renamed the merged company Flowers to emphasise the importance of the keg brand. But Dixon was to learn, as others learnt after him, that companies that grow too quickly attract the attention of even more aggressive and wealthy groups. The result was a merger with Whitbread that was in effect a takeover by the bigger company and escalated what was to become the 'keg war' of the 1960s and 70s.

With the disappearance of J W Green/Flowers into the burgeoning Whitbread empire, Charles Wells could now promote itself as the only independent brewer in Bedfordshire. Trade grew to 34,000 barrels in 1962 and the company introduced its own keg bitter called Noggin.

Two Johns recall brewing times at Horne Lane

John Gibbs

John Gibbs (left) worked for Charles Wells for 36 years and knows the pub trade inside out. Perhaps his greatest achievement was getting Wells's beer into Jesus College in Cambridge, as a result of which a director told him: 'If Jesus loves you, you've got a job for life!'

When John joined the company it was based at Horne Lane and, with so many former army, navy and air force officers as directors or managers, was run like a military establishment. Noggin keg beer had just been introduced and John's nickname was 'Noggin John' as he sold the beer enthusiastically to the pub trade. The beer was important to the company, as all regional brewers were under pressure as a result of the success of Watney's Red Barrel, Double Diamond and other national keg brands.

John is one of the few surviving retired Wells's employees who has vivid memories of Horne Lane. He knew the head brewer Tom Curtis, the only person at Horne Lane who had worked there when Charles Wells was alive.

John remembers the 'nightmare' of attempting to cool wort [unfermented beer] in open vessels before the introduction of paraflow coolers. He recalls coopers with enormous hands and workers in the maltings who were bent almost double from their labours.

Mild ale was the major brand when John started work at the brewery and cost 1s 3d a pint. Noggin keg was priced at 2s a pint. Eagle Bitter was called IPA at the time. The salesmen had to share two cars. The first company car was a Mini, which the driver had to return to the brewery every evening and then go home by bus or bike.

John's most memorable experience was closing a pub in Thurleigh with director Johnny Johnson. When they arrived at the pub, they found the landlord brandishing a shotgun. He held them against the wall and threatened to shoot them. John thought his number was up, but Johnny Johnson, an ex-infantry officer, coolly pushed the gun aside and told the publican: 'We've got a job to do.'

John Stephenson

John Stephenson started work at Charles Wells in the 1960s and still helps out in the company shop. There was no health and safety legislation 50 years ago and John recalls climbing into fermenters that were full of carbon dioxide gas. 'It was good for my singing voice,' he jokes. 'It made me sound like Pavarotti!'

He became brewery foreman and used to start work at 5am in the morning. 'We finished work when we finished the brew. I would come back to the brewery in the evenings 365 days a year to skim the heads' – remove the yeast from the top of the fermenting beer.

John had worked for Scottish & Newcastle before he joined Charles Wells. He remembers fondly the old mash tuns and coppers at Horne Lane, which were sold to Adnams of Southwold when the site closed.

Perhaps as a result of his early, dangerous days cleaning gas-filled fermenters, he is now involved in health and safety training at the brewery as well as running the shop and organising school visits.

There were further encroachments on Wells's trading area. Phipps of Northampton took over Campbell Praed of Wellingborough in 1954 and merged with the Northampton Brewery Co three years later. The two breweries were sited cheek-by-jowl and the merged Phipps NBC celebrated by knocking down the dividing wall. As with J W Green, the enlarged Northampton brewery soon attracted the attention of one of the new national predators. In 1960 Watney Mann – the result of a merger in 1958 – bought Phipps NBC. Watney Mann became owner of 1,200 pubs in Northampton and the surrounding area. In an industry that was starting to resemble the battleground of the Somme in World War One, Charles Wells moved to defend its position. In 1963 it bought the Abington Brewery in Northampton. Abington no longer brewed but the purchase added 23 pubs to the Wells's estate as well as an off-licence and store in Northampton. The purchase boosted Wells's production by 3,000 barrels a year and in 1964 the brewery recorded volumes of 43,000 barrels.

The eagle soars

A new company logo of the Eagle, which was the historic symbol of the town of Bedford, was fixed to all the tied pubs, which numbered more than 300. The company was given a further boost when Noggin won gold and silver medals in the Brewers' Exhibition. The brewery signed a contract with Whitbread to bottle Mackeson Stout, which was a major national brand at that time. Horne Lane was under great pressure as beer volumes grew. When the lease with the borough council on Charles Wells's former home at Newnham House expired, the brewery gratefully took it back for much-needed office space. Malting capacity was expanded in 1965 with a new barley silo while the former Number Two maltings was converted into a fully-palletised bottled beer store. Charter Ale was introduced in 1966 to commemorate the 800th anniversary of Bedford's Charter of 1166: the beer continued to be brewed until 1967.

In the first edition of Charles Wells's company newspaper

THE IMPOSING FAÇADE OF THE
HORNE LANE BREWERY ALONGSIDE
THE RIVER OUSE, DOMINATED BY
ITS SOARING CHIMNEY

RAY SHREEVES SEEN CHECKING BEER IN A CONDITIONING TANK (ABOVE). NEWNHAM HOUSE, ONCE THE HOME OF JOSEPHINE WELLS, WHICH BECAME THE OFFICE FOR HORNE LANE (CENTRE). THE BOTTLING LINE THAT MET THE INSATIABLE DEMAND FOR PACKAGED BEER IN THE 1950S AND 60S IS SEEN ON THE RIGHT WITH FOREMAN IVOR HARRIS

Pint Pot in 1966, Oliver Wells wrote a graphic description of the Horne Lane site. The brewhouse contained malt mills, mash tuns, coppers, hop backs and wort receivers. The fermenting room had eighteen stainless steel fermenters with 40, 80 and 120-barrel capacities. The system was highly flexible, designed so that more than one brew could be undertaken at any time. With annual production running at 45,000 barrels, the importance of keg beer was underscored by chilling tanks, bright beer tanks, and a filling and weighing line. As well as beer, no fewer than seventeen types of mineral water were produced. More than half of malt production was for other companies. So important was malt to Charles Wells that Oliver Wells made an extensive tour of Canada where his brother Sir Charles was a senior executive of the Canada Malting Company. Oliver studied both brewing and malting

in Ontario, Ottawa and Montreal, and crossed the border to visit New York. Back home, only two editions of Pint Pot were produced and the magazine lay dormant until regular production resumed in 1970.

Gaming machines

There were further signs of the changing times in 1967 when Charles Wells, in line with other brewers, introduced gaming machines into pubs as a result of a change in the law on betting and gambling. Both the on and off trades were catered for with a new draught Light Mild and Light Bitter in a take-home can. They were followed by Welcome Brown Ale a year later. A rigorous examination of the tied estate was carried out and a few under-performing pubs were closed. Two new outlets, the Headland in Northampton and the

Dolphin in Bletchley, were built. Total beer sales were close to 50,000 barrels in 1968, the year that John Wells was appointed executive director. He was the son of the late Christopher Wells and was the first grandson of the founder to join the board. After taking a history degree at Cambridge, he qualified as a lawyer and barrister and worked for a shipping association before joining the brewery, where he specialised in sales and also wines and spirits.

Beer sales increased to 52,000 barrels in 1969. The most significant brewing development between 1970 and 1971 was the introduction of Ace Lager, with the Danish Tuborg bottled in Bedford for the company's pubs. The development of the 'holiday package' industry enabled many people to visit mainland Europe, where they sampled lager beer for the first time. From small beginnings in the late 1960s, lager started to

Noggin meets keg challenge

Until Charles Wells introduced Noggin, all its draught beers were cask conditioned, better known to today's consumers as 'real ale'. Cask beers leave the brewery in an unfinished state and reach maturity in cask in the pub cellar as a result of a secondary fermentation. As casks are vented to allow them to breathe and expel some of their natural carbon dioxide, they are open to the atmosphere and the beer will oxidise after a few days.

The first attempt at a keg beer was Watneys Red Barrel, supplied to the East Sheen Tennis Club in Surrey in the 1930s. The club had a slow turnover of cask beer and sold most at weekends. The beer was often in poor condition and the club's members voiced their dissatisfaction. By coincidence, Watneys in London was experimenting with a new type of 'brewery conditioned' draught beer, meant for export to India. The beer was filtered and pasteurised in the brewery, placed in a sealed container called a keg, and impregnated with carbon dioxide gas to give it liveliness and sparkle. Kegs were connected to cylinders of CO_2 in order to drive the beer to the bar.

Watneys diverted some of the supplies of Red Barrel to India via the East Sheen Tennis Club, where it proved a popular success. But sales of keg beer did not take off until the 1960s and early 70s. Large brewers, impressed with the success of filtered bottled beers after the war, took the next step of putting, in effect, bottled beer into kegs. The advantages of keg beer were simple: the inert beer in a sealed container had a shelf life of several months and was therefore more economical and profitable than cask beer.

Red Barrel was followed by Flowers Keg Bitter and soon all the major brewers were producing keg beers. Promoted with expensive and slick advertising, the likes of Allied Breweries' Double Diamond, Bass's Worthington E, Courage's Tankard, Scottish & Newcastle's Tartan, Watneys Red (which replaced Red Barrel), and Whitbread's Flowers and Trophy were immensely successful. Guinness introduced Draught Guinness, which used a mixed gas dispense involving nitrogen as well as CO_2 that resulted in a smoother beer with less carbonic bite. Many smaller breweries did not have the finances to invest in expensive kegging facilities and had to take beer from the majors. Bigger regionals, including Charles Wells, produced their own keg beers, but they never achieved substantial volumes as more and more money was poured into advertising the national brands.

Keg beer's hey-day was relatively brief. When the Campaign for Real Ale was formed in the early 1970s it attacked keg beer as over-priced, over-cold, over-carbonated and under-strength. But the damage had been done. Several thousand cask beers had been phased out in the rush to introduce keg beer.

PUBLIC BAR PRICES

DRAUGHT BEERS					
Mild XX	1/7	pt.	9½d.	half-pt.	
Bitter I.P.A.	1/10	,,	11d.	,,	,,
Noggin Keg Bitter	2/4	,,	1/2d.	,,	,,

BOTTLED BEERS				
Light Ale	-	-	1/2	per bottle
Brown Ale	-	-	1/2	,, ,,
Bowman Stout	-	-	1/3	,, ,,
Double Star	-	-	1/4	,, ,,
Fargo Strong Ale	-	-	1/7	,, ,,
Old Bedford Ale	-	-	1/7½	,, nip
Charter Ale	-	-	1/8	per bottle
Guinness	-	-	1/7½	,, ,,
Lager — Harp	-	-	1/7½	,, ,,
Lager — Tuborg	-	-	1/10¼	,, ,,
Double Diamond	-	-	1/8½	,, ,,
Mackeson Stout	-	-	1/8	,, ,,
Worthington Green	-	-	1/8½	,, ,,
Worthington White	-	-	1/10¼	,, ,,

CHARLES WELLS LTD.

25th JULY, 1966

THE FIRST KEG BEER, WATNEY'S RED BARREL, WAS FOLLOWED

BY FLOWERS AND SOON ALL THE NATIONALS HAD KEG BRANDS

change the face of the British brewing industry. In common with many regional brewers, Charles Wells's first attempt at a European-style beer was known by the somewhat derogatory name of 'bastard lager'. The Horne Lane site was a traditional ale brewery and did not have such facilities as decoction mashing, which requries several mashing vessels, and lautering (mash filtration) enjoyed by Belgian, Dutch, German and Czech brewers. Ace Lager was, in effect, a keg pale ale produced by warm fermentation with an ale yeast, and served suitably chilled in pubs. But at least Ace avoided some of the risible names used by other regional brewers, such as Brock from the Badger brewery, Grunhalle (brewed by Greenall Whitley), Norseman, Regal, which is lager spelt backwards, and a clutch of brand names ending in -brau, the German for 'brew', of which Hibrau was possibly the most memorably awful. Most of the first wave of lagers quickly disappeared. The regional brewers were to learn that lager sales were driven by advertising and consumers peferred the comfort blanket of such household brands as Carlsberg,

THE 'SWINGING 60S' SAW NEW STYLES OF ADVERTISING, INCLUDING THE POP ART BUS (ABOVE LEFT) AND A VERY JOLLY SAILOR ENJOYING NOGGIN BITTER. THE PRICE LIST (LEFT) SHOWS THE WIDE RANGE OF BEERS AVAILABLE IN A WELLS'S PUB

JOHN WELLS BECAME EXECUTIVE DIRECTOR IN 1968. HE WAS THE GREAT GRANDSON OF THE FOUNDER AND WAS INSTRUMENTAL IN BUILDING SALES BOTH AT HOME AND IN OVERSEAS MARKETS

Carling, Heineken and Tuborg, even if they were brewed under licence in Britain and often bore little resemblance to the genuine article.

The 1970s began with further expansion of the brewery. A new mash tun and two stainless steel fermenters were installed to increase capacity while plans were drawn up for a new fermenting room and keg beer tank room. Ambitious plans to buy a pub in Paris fell through, but Charles Wells would eventually build a presence in the French capital. Horace Tebbs, who had been Company Secretary since 1954, became a non-executive director, and John Wells took over as secretary. A Friden computer was bought in 1970 and, reflecting the development and advantages of new technology, a computer room was built a year later in order that the company could modernise the storage and handling of sales, raw material, salaries and wages. As a further sign of changing consumer demand, the company set up a star rating system for food in its tied estate, which now numbered 270 pubs. High standards were set for food and 59 pubs qualified to display a 'Good Food' plaque, with a rating from one to four stars.

ABC rejected

Charles Wells was once again forced to consider its position as the result of restructuring of the brewing industry. The Aylesbury Brewery Company (ABC) had ceased brewing in 1937 and operated as a retail estate, with beers supplied by other brewers. By 1971, Allied Breweries, formed by a merger of Allsopp, Ind Coope and Tetley, owned 40 per cent of ABC's shares. Allied was expected to bid for the remainder of the shares, and ABC proposed to Morrells Brewery of Oxford and Charles Wells that the three should form a new public company. Allied would control 13.5 per cent of the equity. The Charles Wells board saw many disadvantages from such an arrangement. In the end, nothing came of the proposals and Allied made a successful offer for ABC's remaining shares in 1972, and added some prime Home Counties and Thames Valley pubs to its national estate.

EVERYONE'S FAVOURITE...EXCEPT WELLS FARGO BANK IN THE UNITED STATES. THE BEER WAS WITHDRAWN FOR A WHILE UNTIL THE DISPUTE WAS AMICABLY SETTLED

The Charles Wells's beer range in 1972 was made up of cask Mild and IPA, keg Noggin and Ace Lager, with bottled Light Ale, Brown Ale, Welcome Brown Ale, Bowman Stout, Double Star, Fargo Strong Ale, and Old Bedford Ale. A new keg beer, Golden Eagle Bitter, was launched and emphasised the company's commitment to the ale sector. Horne Lane also supplied its pubs with bottled and draught Guinness, Double Diamond, Worthington E and White Shield, Mackeson Stout, and Harp and Tuborg lagers. Light Ale won a silver medal at the Brewers' Exhibition that year.

When Thomas Curtis retired from the company in 1971 after a remarkable 73 years' service, he did so at a time when Charles Wells was about to undergo a period of tumultuous change. Malt was still being made for Guinness at the start of the year but, after a review of costs and budgets, and continuing pressure on production space, the board took the decision to stop malting. From then on, and in common with most other brewers at the time, Charles Wells bought in its grain requirements from specialist malting companies. The head maltster, Mr Lindsay-White, transferred to the brewery. A year later, when Jonathan Harrison was appointed financial director and the company was shocked by the early death at 56 of John Redman, the wines and spirits manager, the search began for a new head brewer to replace R O Gorman, who was due to retire. The search took the better part of a year and resulted in the appointment in November of Roy Morewood, who was to play a pivotal role in the changes to come. Morewood had started his brewing career as a pupil – the industry's term for an apprentice – at Hyde's Anvil Brewery in

The Jackal, Thurleigh
Kevin and Julia Hanks

Julia and Kevin Hanks have turned the badly neglected Jackal at Thurleigh into an award-winning pub. They worked for a short time in other pubs before taking over the village local in 1998. It dates from the 17th century and was a Jarvis outlet before it was bought by Wells. The current name is a corruption of Jacks' Hall: before it became a pub it was the village blacksmith's and washhouse.

The Hanks say the Jackal was in a dreadful state when they arrived. It had been a flagship pub but had declined as a result of a rapid turnover of tenants. With financial help from the brewery, Julia and Kevin installed new carpets, curtains and dishwashers, and had the pub decorated.

Kevin is a professional chef and has used his skills to build the food side, which now account for 60 per cent of their trade. The Hanks are adamant, however, that the Jackal is a pub that serves food, not a restaurant. They run monthly themed food events and also provide takeaway meals for commuters who can phone their orders from their trains.

The major change in drinking habits is a move from beer to wine. Wine sales have increased by 20 per cent a year as beer has declined. The Hanks say it is the disappearance of farmers and their workers that has led to the loss of beer sales. In 2000 and 2001, the Hanks won the coveted Tenanted Pub of the Year award from the Morning Advertiser weekly trade newspaper.

Manchester. He worked for two more breweries before settling at James Hole's Castle Brewery in Newark, where he left as head brewer. He arrived at Horne Lane to find the site under great pressure from increasing volumes of beer. The old malting plant was broken up to release additional space, but it was becoming increasingly clear that Horne Lane, for all its historic importance to the company, was becoming a fetter on future development.

The company's arm was forced in 1973. Bedford Council told the directors in confidential talks that it needed land on which the Horne Lane site stood for a riverside walk. It offered in exchange some land at Batts Ford. The directors realised that no further expansion was possible at Horne Lane and another location was urgently needed for bottling and warehousing. An eleven-acre site at Queens Park, owned by Eastern Gas, was earmarked. The board was dismayed when their plans were leaked to the Bedfordshire Times. The paper reported that negotiations were taking place to sell Horne Lane to the council for £1,250,000 while Charles Wells planned to build a new brewery near Bedford Town FC's ground. Eastern Gas agreed that it had been approached about selling its site but said no agreement had been reached. A second report in the Bedfordshire Times added fuel to the flames. It was written by Frank Branston, an energetic campaigning journalist who was later to found his own independent newspaper, Bedford on Sunday. Branston reported that a row was brewing as the sum of £1,250,000 was double the price previously paid in Bedford for development land. He also claimed that talks between Charles Wells and Eastern Gas were well advanced, contrary to what the gas corporation had said the previous week. The directors knew they had to act quickly to calm the situation, and to quash rumours that were potentially damaging to all the contending parties. After protracted discussions, the board took the bold decision – unprecedented among regional brewers at the time – to leave Horne Lane, sell the site to the council, and build a new brewery at Queens Park. The financial arrangements were negotiated with the Midland Bank, and the decision to proceed was finally taken in October 1973 to go ahead with what was enigmatically entitled, in the manner of a Robert Ludlum novel, The Southgate Project.

THE ROYAL OAK AT CARLTON, A VIBRANT EXAMPLE OF A MODERN, WELCOMING WELLS'S PUB. ABOVE, PRESS HEADLINES IN THE 1970S THAT LEAKED THE PLANNED BREWERY MOVE TO A NEW SITE

A new brewery, a new era

THE EAGLE BREWERY, A MODERN, IMPRESSIVE BUT essentially functional office and brewery complex at the end of Havelock Street in Bedford, was officially opened on 18 May 1976 by the Duke of Gloucester. Few people who attended the celebrations were aware of the problems in creating the new brewery that at times seemed insuperable and drove strong men if not to drink but close to despair.

Three years earlier, in October 1972, Oliver Wells had been put in charge of the Southgate Project. Central to the plan was the need to create a modern and flexible brewery that could produce 100,000 barrels of beer a year. Horne Lane was creaking at every seam and joist as production in 1974 was increased to 70,000 barrels to keep pace with demand. Equipment was not neglected, however, with new vessels added to give the brewery three mash tuns, three coppers and twenty-one stainless steel fermenters. The final range of beers produced on the original site were XX Mild, IPA Bitter, Noggin Bitter, Gold Eagle Bitter, Silver Eagle Light Bitter and Ace Lager

in draught form, with Light, Brown, Welcome Brown, Double Star, Fargo, Ace and Old Bedford Ale in bottle. John Wells became sales director and the annual advertising budget was increased from £25,000 to £30,000.

Roy Morewood, whose tenure as head brewer straddled old and new sites, gives a graphic image of Horne Lane in its final days. He marked his arrival by tripping over a steep final step into the brewers' office and fell flat on his face. It was an ignominious start for a man hired to lead the company into a new era, but he recovered from his early fall from grace by the vigour and determination of his leadership. Horne Lane was a traditional tower brewery, with the brewing processes flowing from floor to floor without the need for mechanical pumps. The plant was driven by steam power, with belts running rotary shafts. Morewood straight away changed one aspect of cask beer production. Until he arrived, beer was racked straight from the fermenters into cask, which Morewood was convinced could lead to poor quality. Instead he ran the beer

THE MODERN FACE OF THE NEW BREWERY IN HAVELOCK STREET. LEFT, THE BREWING PROCESS IS COMPUTER CONTROLLED BY KEITH HINDE. RIGHT, HOPS ARE ADDED BY PHIL BREWER TO THE BREW KETTLE AND ARE BOILED WITH THE WORT

from fermenters into racking tanks, where it rested for a few days and purged itself of unwanted rough alcohols. He recalls that in 1974 bottled beer accounted for a quarter of Charles Wells's production though volumes were beginning to decline. Mild on draught and in bottle was also going into long and eventually terminal free-fall.

Critical water supply

Oliver Wells is another leading player from 1976 who has instant recall where the switch from old to new brewery is concerned. Water or 'brewing liquor' is the lifeblood of any brewery. It was of critical importance that consumers should not be able to detect any change in the flavour of Wells's beers.

This meant that identical water was needed at Havelock Street with the correct balance of natural salts, such as gypsum and magnesium, that enhance the flavours of malt and hops. Oliver Wells's task was to negotiate the piping of water from the main running alongside the river bank at Horne Lane site to Havelock Street.

It became clear to the directors that there was scope for a bigger site at Havelock Street than they had thought. Bedford Town FC's ground stood next to the old Eastern Gas works. As the football club was going bankrupt, Charles Wells would eventually be able to get the sports ground as well for much-needed warehousing. But the immediate problem was the poor state of the land at the new site, which had not been

OLIVER WELLS IS SEEN LEFT ON
THE 'RAFT' THAT WAS BUILT AS
THE BASE FOR THE NEW
BREWERY AT HAVELOCK
STREET. BEYOND IS BEDFORD
TOWN'S FOOTBALL GROUND
THAT WAS LATER TO BECOME
PART OF THE BREWERY SITE

RIGHT, VEHICLES ARRIVE AT
HAVELOCK STREET TO INSTALL
NEW BREWING VESSELS AND
EQUIPMENT. THE SITE WAS
DESIGNED SO THAT
EQUIPMENT COULD BE
LOWERED THROUGH THE ROOF

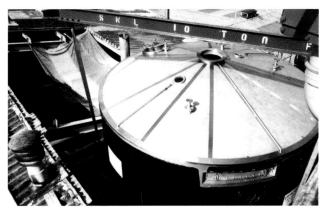

detected by early surveys. Years of gas production had contaminated the sub-soil with the extracts from coke and coal. The sub-soil was also unstable and plans for piled foundations had to be abandoned. The ground had to be dug out to a depth of one-and-a-half metres and filled with concrete. In Roy Morewood's telling phrase, the new brewery was built on a giant concrete raft, which added considerably to the costs. He worked closely with Gordon Smith and Partners, experienced engineers who had also carried out work for several other regional brewers. Hugh Hughes and the Charles Wells architects department were responsible for the bulk of the planning work. The building work was carried out by J M Hill of Ampthill, who constructed a large steel-framed

Recorded on site

The new site at Havelock Street included a building where Glenn Miller played his last concert to American and British troops in World War Two before the bandleader disappeared during a flight to France. The building was dubbed The Shrine.

Miller has a bronze bust in the Corn Exchange. His military orchestra was based in Bedford during the war and they made many of their morale-boosting broadcasts to troops in the town. The studios in Havelock Street, known as Co-Partners Hall, where the broadcasts were made were demolished to make way for the Eagle Centre at Charles Wells's Brewery in 2002. Bing Crosby and Dinah Shore were two of several American singing stars who recorded in Bedford with the Miller Army Airforce Band.

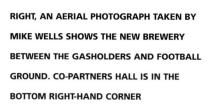

RIGHT, AN AERIAL PHOTOGRAPH TAKEN BY MIKE WELLS SHOWS THE NEW BREWERY BETWEEN THE GASHOLDERS AND FOOTBALL GROUND. CO-PARTNERS HALL IS IN THE BOTTOM RIGHT-HAND CORNER

building in which brewing and fermentation were carried out at one end, followed by filtration, cask, keg and bottle filling, and finally a storage and loading bay. The areas that supplied steam, water and power were located in the centre of the building. Oliver Wells wanted what he called a 'barn-like structure' in order that the roof could be removed if new plant needed to be installed. Doorways were enormous to allow easy access by drays and trucks.

Once the problems with the foundations were solved, work on the new site progressed smoothly. Horne Lane could not close one day and Havelock Street open the next: the two sites

had to work in tandem for several months. As an entirely new method of fermenting beer was planned for Havelock Street, the brewery knew it could have a problem with both publicans and drinkers. Roy Morewood had argued powerfully for a flexible system of fermentation that used upright, enclosed conical vessels in place of the open horizontal ones at Horne Lane. He was keen to move away from the tower system as he believed wort, the essential sugary extract produced by mashing grain and water, should not be pumped from floor to floor. At Havelock Street, it would be possible to pump it horizontally on just one level.

Oliver Wells recalls that the brewery's licensees were convinced the beer would taste different. To reassure them, beer was brewed at the new site, trunked to Horne Lane and then delivered to the pubs. Nobody complained nor spotted any flavour differences, let alone the slight deception that had been played on them.

There was considerable sadness among older members of staff as Horne Lane – the creation so many years ago of Charles Wells – neared its end. Newnham House was vacated in September 1975, with the remainder of the site due to be cleared by the middle of January of the following year. The registered offices moved to Abington House in Havelock Street in November 1975. Horne Lane was demolished in 1976, including the Harpur Arms pub that dated from 1836. The final symbolic act took place on 22 November when a controlled explosion demolished the 84-year-old, 120-foot brewery chimney. Only Newnham House remained. It stood empty until 1980 when it, too, was demolished and was replaced by a housing association. The entire brewery site is now a riverside car park with a market held on Wednesdays and Saturdays.

The Eagle Brewery cost £3,600,000, more than one million

pounds over budget. The overspend was caused mainly by the problems with the sub-soil and the need to build the concrete raft. The site cost £1 million, buildings and plant £2.6 million and the unbudgeted removal of subsoil £300,000. Nevertheless, the new brewery was a revelation. No other regional brewer of comparable size to Charles Wells had contemplated taking such a giant step from traditional ale brewing to a highly flexible site that could produce cask and keg ale as well as lager. But these were challenging times. The History of the British Brewing Industry by T R Gourvish and R G Wilson (Cambridge, 1994) calls the period between the mid 1950s and the early 80s 'Merger Mania'. Larger regional brewers had amalgamated to form what were known as the Big Six national groups: Allied Breweries, Bass Charrington, Courage, Watney Mann & Truman, Whitbread, and Scottish & Newcastle. The mergers that created these groups led to scores

NO OTHER REGIONAL BREWERY

HAD CONTEMPLATED TAKING

SUCH A GIANT STEP FROM

TRADITIONAL ALE BREWING TO

A MODERN, FLEXIBLE SITE

of small breweries closing down. The total number of national beer brands dropped by half, from 3,000 to 1,500. The Big Six were interested in keg and lager brands that could be promoted nationally, on commercial television in particular. The biggest brewing group, Bass Charrington, had been created by a Canadian E P (Eddie) Taylor, who owned Carling Black Label lager and was determined to control sufficient brewing capacity in Britain to make it the top brand. Whitbread had embarked on a scheme known as the 'umbrella', under which the national company took minority shareholdings in a number of regional brewers with a view to defending them against future takeovers. But these proved to be Faustian pacts, and many of the breweries that huddled under the giant umbrella were eventually swallowed and closed by the very company that had offered to save them.

With regional and smaller family-owned breweries falling like ninepins, the Charles Wells's directors knew that survival lay in brewing a wide portfolio of beers to suit all tastes, to have the flexibility to brew ale and lager alongside one another, and to undertake contract brewing for other companies. The directors also saw that the rise of the supermarket chains and a trend for consumers to drink at home as well as in the pub made it necessary to produce packaged beer in both cans and bottles. Significantly, the first new beer brewed at Havelock Street was Kellerbrau, a lager brewed in the proper European manner and employing a true lager yeast. For once the German tag -brau (brew) was not

THERE SHE GOES...
MEMORABLE PHOTOGRAPHS
CAPTURE THE END OF THE
HORNE LANE CHIMNEY,
BLOWN UP AS THE ENTIRE
SITE WAS DEMOLISHED.
INSET, THE DATE WHEN THE
CHIMNEY WAS BUILT

How beer is brewed at Charles Wells

The Eagle Brewery is highly flexible. It runs on two brew lines and can produce seven 'worts' – sugary extracts – every twenty-four hours. In a traditional ale brewery, a mash tun is used to produce wort by a simple infusion mash: the same vessel also filters the mash. The Charles Wells's plant is based on the European model, with mash mixers linked to filtration vessels known as lauter tuns. Separating mashing from filtering means that more brews can be processed during the course of a shift.

When lager is produced, the brewhouse uses a temperature programme system. The mash mixers are fitted with jackets heated by steam to raise the temperature. Mashing starts at 48-50°C, then the temperature is raised in steps to 76°C. If the recipe calls for other grains to be used, such as maize or rice, they are prepared in a cereal cooker before being added to the main barley mash.

During mashing, protein in the cereal breaks down, allowing natural enzymes to convert starch into fermentable malt sugar or maltose. This conversion is known as saccharification and takes place at 65°C. The final temperature of 76°C is too high for saccharification to continue and kills the enzymes. The mash is pumped to the lauter tun, which has a slotted base. The grain settles on the base and the liquid wort filters through it, picking up any remaining valuable malt sugars as it is sparged with brewing water.

Boil with hops

The wort is then boiled vigorously with hops in the copper or brew-kettle. During the boil, vital oils, tannins and resins are extracted from the hops that add aroma and bitterness to beer. At the end of the boil, the hopped wort is separated from the spent hops by a whirlpool action, and cooled prior to fermentation, which takes place in upright conical vessels. Charles Wells uses special strains of yeast for each lager beer it brews in order to maintain the correct balance of flavours. Primary fermentation for lager starts at around 8°C, which rises as a result of the heat created as yeast transforms malt sugars into alcohol and carbon dioxide. Refrigerant is pumped through jackets on the fermenters to maintain the temperature at around 12°C. Fermentation continues for up to fourteen days, after which the unfinished or 'green' beer is transferred to conditioning tanks where it is stored (the German word is 'lager' or storage place) for a maximum of seventy days, depending on which beer is being produced. The temperature is held at 2-5°C then lowered at the end of the lagering period to -1°C. The beer is filtered to remove the deposit of yeast and protein left in the conditioning tank, and is then ready to be racked into kegs or run into bottles and cans.

Charles Wells's ales, Eagle and Bombardier in particular, are brewed using the same equipment but by a modified method using a single step temperature increase. Ale malt is described as 'fully modified', which means the changes inside the grain that allow starch to be turned into fermentable maltose are fully developed.

Lager malts, on the other hand, traditionally used by European brewers, are less developed and require a more exhaustive mashing regime to finish modification.

out of place as the beer was made by true cold fermentation.

More than 80,000 barrels were brewed in the first year at Havelock Street. A new beer, Century Lager, was produced, while Fargo was made available in draught form. Roy Morewood took particular care with the cask-conditioned beers. He found that, as a result of the new method of fermentation, they contained too much yeast when racked into cask. He devised a system whereby the beers were centrifuged to remove the yeast and were then 're-seeded' with the correct amount of yeast to ensure a good, natural secondary fermentation in cask. The result was consistent beers that dropped bright quickly in pubs and were known as 'landlord friendly'. The emphasis on cask beer was essential. The Campaign for Real Ale (CAMRA) had been formed in 1971 and was vigorously promoting traditional draught beer. The renewed interest in the style saw a dramatic increase in sales at Charles Wells, with draught volumes overtaking those of bright products. CAMRA took a long, hard look at Wells's methods of producing cask beer. Some members queried whether a beer that was filtered and then re-seeded with yeast was natural or 'real'.

CHEERS! A SPECIAL LAGER WAS BREWED TO MARK A CENTURY OF BREWING IN BEDFORD

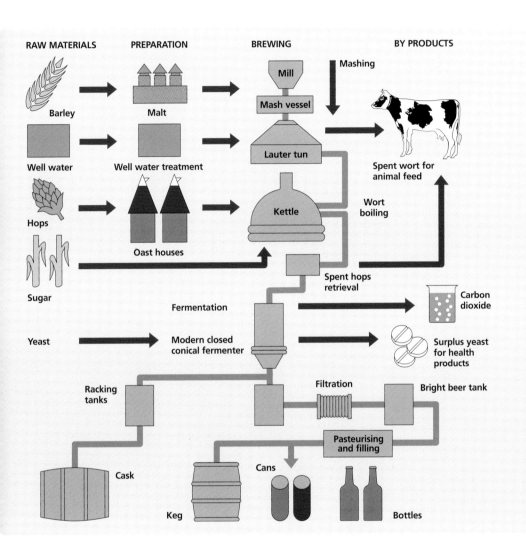

RAW MATERIALS — Barley, Well water, Hops, Sugar, Yeast

PREPARATION — Malt, Well water treatment, Oast houses

BREWING — Mill, Mash vessel, Lauter tun, Kettle, Mashing, Wort boiling, Fermentation, Modern closed conical fermenter, Racking tanks, Filtration, Bright beer tank, Pasteurising and filling, Cask, Keg, Cans, Bottles

BY PRODUCTS — Spent wort for animal feed, Spent hops retrieval, Carbon dioxide, Surplus yeast for health products

For ale, the mashing process takes place in the same vessels as lager but does not use the first low temperature phase, starting at the conversion or saccharifaction temperature around 65°, when conversion is complete after 90 minutes. Steam jackets raise the temperature to 76° before it is transfered to the lauter tun. The wort is filtered in the lauter tun and pumped to the kettle, where it is boiled with ale hop varieties, used for their intense bitterness, and spicy, resiny aroma. The hopped wort is cooled and pumped to conical fermenters where an ale yeast culture is pitched. Ale yeast works at a higher temperature than lager yeast. Fermentation rises from 18°C to 22°C and lasts for around seven to eight days. The green beer then stands in racking tanks for a few days where the amount of yeast present is stabilised, and finings and additional hops for aroma are added.

When conical vessels are used, the yeast settles at the base of the vessel in a similar manner to lager yeast. The Well's ale yeast is recultured frequently to maintain consistency and quality.

But the objections were quickly withdrawn and the brewery has long enjoyed excellent relations with the campaign at both local and national level.

Packaged beers were not neglected. A joint venture known as the Jarvis Canning Company was set up with Ruddles Brewery of Oakham in Rutland. Ruddles – controversially – had sold all but one of its tied pubs to concentrate on packaged beers for supermarkets, but its cramped site in England's smallest county didn't offer sufficient space for a canning line. Wells, on the other hand, now had a 'Legoland' site designed with expansion in mind, and it went into partnership with Ruddles determined to make inroads into the growing take-home sector. The directors became ever more conscious of the need to sell their products. They sought maximum publicity through national and local press as well as television. The house magazine Pint Pot had been relaunched in 1970 and has appeared several times a year since then, ending its run in 2002 when it was replaced by Eagle Eye, a new newspaper for a new century.

Red Stripe boost

Soon after the opening of Havelock Street, an offer was made to Charles Wells that was to vindicate the decision to build the new site and offer flexible brewing facilities. Peter Shardlow, a leading Whitbread executive, visited the Desnoes & Geddes Brewery in Jamaica, where the leading lager brand in the Caribbean, Red Stripe, was produced. Paul Geddes, a director of the brewery, suggested to Shardlow that Whitbread might

THE IMPRESSIVE NEW
BREWHOUSE AT HAVELOCK
STREET, WHERE BOTH ALES AND
LAGERS CAN BE
PRODUCED, WITH SEVERAL
NEW BREWS A DAY

THE BREWING COPPERS (LEFT)
WHERE THE SUGARY EXTRACT
OR WORT IS BOILED WITH HOPS
TO GIVE THE LIQUID AROMA
AND BITTERNESS

TALL FERMENTATION TANKS
OUTSIDE THE BREWHOUSE
WHERE SEVERAL BREWS ARE
COLLECTED FOR FERMENTATION

ABOVE, THE CASK RACKING LINE,
WHERE EAGLE AND BOMBARDIER
ARE RUN INTO CASKS BY
LORENZO BAIO PRIOR
TO DELIVERY TO PUBS. BECAUSE
OF THE SIZE OF THE BREWERY,
THE BEERS ARE FILTERED, PIPED
TO THE RACKING AREA
AND RE-SEEDED WITH YEAST TO
ENSURE A GOOD SECOND
FERMENTATION

THE VAST PACKAGING LINES
WHERE VERSIONS OF BOTH ALE
AND LAGER ARE MADE READY
FOR DOMESTIC AND
INTERNATIONAL SALES

consider brewing Red Stripe under licence in Britain. When he mentioned a possible volume of 15,000 barrels a year, Shardlow said it was too small for Whitbread to take on, and recommended that Geddes approach Charles Wells. This was just the opportunity Wells was looking for. As Roy Morewood recalls, there were no premium lagers in Britain at the time, and Red Stripe was an immediate success. Whitbread must have cursed a lost opportunity when production of Red Stripe at Bedford eventually peaked at 130,000 barrels. A new company called Red Stripe Marketing was created to handle distribution and promotion of the brand. Charles Wells at first had a 20 per cent stake in the company, but over the following years the company would increase its stake until it eventually became half owner of Red Stripe in Britain.

Red Stripe proved an exciting challenge for Roy Morewood and his team, a challenge that was to hold them in good stead as new lager contracts were won. Yeast was imported from Jamaica and the original recipe was faithfully followed. This required buying the American hop variety Cluster, which has a pungent citrus aroma but low bitterness. The full, rich palate of the beer is achieved by adding maize syrup to the malting barley. Charles Wells added a cereal cooker in the early 1980s in order that grains other than barley could be prepared separately and then added to the mash mixers.

David Wells retired as an executive on 31 January 1978, but remained as chairman. Oliver Wells was appointed chief executive and vice-chairman, while John Wells became deputy chief executive and marketing director. Roy Morewood was promoted to the post of technical director and head brewer. It proved to be a year of dramatic developments. The workforce at Havelock Street grew to 180 in brewing, warehousing, packaging, administration and sales. The planned capacity of 100,000 barrels was reached and in November an all-time monthly record of 2,700 barrels were brewed. More tied pubs were bought and an 18th-century farmhouse was converted into the Barley Mow

SALES OF RED STRIPE DROVE THE NEW BREWERY AND MADE A SECOND BREWHOUSE NECESSARY. PACKAGING INCLUDES BOTH LONG NECK AND SHORT NECK BOTTLES AND CANS, PLUS A SMART DRAUGHT DISPENSE. ADVERTISING IN 2004 MADE USE OF THE JAMAICAN PATOIS

in Hartford, Cambridgeshire. Kellerbrau won a first prize for lager in a competition staged by the British Bottlers Institute in London. A sad note was struck by the death of Henry McRae in June in a four-vehicle crash at Moggerhanger. He had joined the brewery in 1960 and was the director responsible for tied houses. James Baker, with a wide experience in the pub trade since 1948, joined as estate manager. As part of a programme of opening the brewery to visitors, two guides, Sue Holloway and Wendy Evans, were appointed.

Output doubled

The first financial report issued to shareholders in 1979 reported a turnover of £15,600,000, compared to £5,900,000 in the final year at Horne Lane. Output virtually doubled, from 60,000 barrels to 119,000. In line with the aims of the directors, contract brewing, bottling and canning represented 30 per cent of production. A profit-sharing scheme for employees was introduced and the company paid £145,000 in to a non-contributory pension fund. Dr Christopher Wells, son of Sir Charles Wells, became a non-executive director, and Jonathan Harrison, a non-executive director, joined the board as financial director. David Wells retired as chairman after 24 years and became the company's first president. Oliver Wells, the new chairman, reported that financing of the new brewery was almost entirely paid off, a remarkable achievement in such a short period. A 75 per cent stake was purchased in V Arbuckle & Co, a London beer and wine wholesalers, which marked the start of a determined effort by Charles Wells to build a presence in the capital.

The Anchor & Hope in Southwark, bought the following year, was Wells's first London pub. To cut losses, the Arbuckle warehouse was closed but the value of the company was critical in allowing Wells to develop sales to pubs and off-licences in London. Beer, wines and spirits from then on were supplied from Bedford, with an order office at Park Royal in North-west London. The stake in Arbuckle was increased to

100 per cent and the name was changed to Charles Wells Marketing Ltd, but losses continued due to poor management and the company was eventually wound up. At the same time, the company increased its shareholding in Red Stripe Marketing to 45 per cent and the famous West Country cider maker, HP Bulmer, which also wholesaled beer and cider to all parts of the country, was appointed as the sole distributor of packaged Red Stripe in Britain to take advantage of their national distribution network.

A turning point in Charles Wells's draught ale production was marked in 1980 by the introduction of Bombardier premium bitter. Named after the famous pre-war boxer Bombardier Billy Wells, who had no connection with the family, the beer was to become the linchpin of the brewery's ale production. It was eventually to become one of the biggest-selling premium bitters in Britain and would drive Wells's success in the free trade. In stronger forms, it became an important part of the company's export initiative.

Changes on the board

Commander Milburn died in 1981 after 23 years as a non-executive director. He joined the company in 1954 as a manager before going on to the board. He had a family connection as he married Mary Wells, daughter of Sir Richard, in 1938. James Baker was promoted to estates director, while Tom Wells, the son of David, joined the brewery as orders office manager and began to develop what was then a new concept of telesales with the aid of computers. Tom Wells was educated at Shiplake College and Shuttleworth College. He worked for a grain trading and shipping firm before joining Munton & Fison, where he deepened his knowledge of the malting processes.

The London order office at Park Royal was closed in 1981 as a result of financial losses at Charles Wells Marketing. On the positive side, Jarvis Canning made a sound contribution to company profits as a result of contract bottling and canning. Eventually, Charles Wells bought out Ruddles and became the sole owner of Jarvis, which is now known as Jarvis Solutions. The ever-increasing popularity for Red Stripe led to the decision to produce the lager in draught form for the on-trade.

Turnover increased in 1982. 160,000 barrels were brewed

MODERN PUB, TRADITIONAL FORMS OF TRANSPORT... CUSTOMERS ARRIVE ON HORSEBACK AT THE SWAN INN AT RADWELL

THE BREWERY PRODUCED A SPECIAL BOTTLED WEDDING ALE IN 1981 TO MARK THE WEDDING OF PRINCE CHARLES AND PRINCESS DIANA

but, in a fiercely competitive beer market, there was pressure on profits. The difficult trading times did not deter Wells from increasing its presence in London, though, where two further pubs were bought. Closer to home, the Pheasant opened on the Kimbolton Road estate in Bedford, designed by Hugh Hughes. Investment was stepped up in the brewery with the addition of new fermenting vessels and a carbon dioxide recovery plant: the CO2 plant reduced the purchase of gas by a quarter. When the lease on Bedford Town FC's ground adjoining the brewery expired, Charles Wells moved on to the 5.5 acre site. The old North Stand of the football ground is used as a hop store and also houses offices for Technical Services. With its sloping roof, the building from the outside still looks like an old-fashioned soccer stand.

A Tenants' Association for Charles Wells's licensees was set up in 1978, and the Century pub had a training facility installed for trainee managers, prospective tenants and free trade customers. A popular new marketing tool arrived in the shape of barrel-shaped hot air balloon, which was registered as G-PINT. It was flown at major events in Befordshire and surrounding counties, and also featured in television commercials. The balloon appeared on the cover of a booklet, Eagle Country, published in 1983, which included photos of pubs and a tour of what was calld 'Charles Wells Country'. Paul Wells, the son of Oliver Wells, joined the company in 1984 as area sales manager for London. The year was marked by Jarvis Canning, run by Ray Shreeves, filling 36 million cans and 40 million bottles.

The tied estate increased in 1984 with the purchase of three new pubs. The opening of a new shopping centre in Cambridge led to the demolition of the Ancient Druids, but a new pub with the same name was built close by. The new version of the Ancient Druids had its own small brewery

attached at a cost of £250,000. In-house breweries had become popular features of the pub trade as a result of the success of the Firkin chain of home-brew pubs launched in the late 1970s by David Bruce.

New opportunities

There were changes at boardroom level that year. Oliver Wells retired as chief executive after 28 years with the company, and John Wells stepped up to replace him. Oliver continued to serve the brewery as non-executive chairman, while Tom Wells became marketing manager. The company looked for new opportunities in the free trade and appointed a wholesaler for South Wales in addition to the Midlands, East Anglia and London. The company also began to look abroad and beer was exported from 1980 onwards, first to

THE OLD NORTH STAND OF THE

FOOTBALL GROUND IS USED AS

A HOP STORE AND OFFICE FOR

THE TECHNICAL SERVICES TEAM

the United States and then to Italy. Italy was to prove fertile ground: in a country best known for wine making and consumption, consumers responded surprisingly well to strong English ales. Brewery expansion continued with the addition of a new filtration unit, bright beer tanks and a malt-handling plant. The following year, 1985, a new wines and spirits bonded store was completed while sales of Red Stripe on draught and in packaged form reached 35,000 barrels. Anthony Wallis, now retail director, joined the company from Bateman's Brewery in Lincolnshire, taking over the London sales region from Paul Wells.

Pressure on profits from sales to supermarkets were the result of increased competition, but the situation improved the following year, and rising sales of packaged beers again put a strain on production facilities. New pubs, the Roman Legion

in Luton, and the Dog & Duck in Houghton Regis, were opened, while Talisman low alcohol lager and Ensign Bitter were introduced. Both turnover and profits increased in 1987 and the substantial sum of £750,000 was invested in additional brewing, fermenting and conditioning equipment as well as a central cleaning plant. In a year of intense business activity, the Broughton Hotel close to the M1 motorway was opened and more pubs were added to the estate. £2 million was raised by selling some properties, and the money was re-invested in the existing estate. Nineteen pubs were bought from the break-up of the Grand Metropolitan estate.

The importance of Bombardier Bitter to the company was boosted when the beer won the top prize at the Le Monde Séléction International beer competition in Brussels. This followed an award for best beer at the Brewing Industry

THE CHANGING FACE OF
BOMBARDIER...HOW THE
PUMP CLIPS HAVE ALTERED
TO MIRROR MODERN
TASTES AND IMAGES

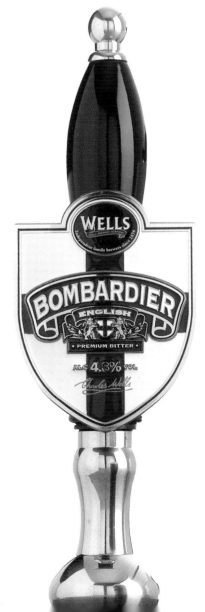

**ROY MOREWOOD (CENTRE) SEEN BEARING A CUP
TO MARK ONE OF THE BREWERY'S MANY VICTORIES
IN BREWING COMPETITIONS. BELOW, DOUBLE STAR
WAS A WINNER AT BREWEX IN 1983**

International Awards in Britain. Red Stripe and Talisman also won awards in their classes. As a harbinger of what was to be known as the 'guest beer' policy of the 1990s, Charles Wells and Mansfield Brewery near Nottingham reached a trading agreement that resulted in Mansfield's Marksman lager being made available to Wells's pubs while Red Stripe went on sale in Mansfield outlets.

There was a dramatic expansion of the pub estate in 1988, which grew from 283 to 306. Nineteen pubs were bought, along with two hotels, the Old Bull in Royston and the Old Falcon in St Neots. A new delivery warehouse was completed along with automated lines for both cask and keg beer filling. Eagle LA was added to Talisman in the low alcohol sector. Johnny Johnson died aged 64 just before he was due to retire as the result of falling from a ladder. He joined the brewery's transport department in 1947 after military service but soon moved on to become Sales Manager and then Free Trade Manager. His last position was Technical Services Manager.

One of his first jobs in the brewery had been to act as a relief driver for Sir Richard Wells. In a busy year of new appointments, Tom Wells became marketing director and was also responsible for public relations, while Toby Dobson became sales director. Paul Wells was appointed national accounts manager with a team of regional sales executives, to build national sales of Red Stripe and Bombardier. Hot air balloons were joined by an airship, Skyship 600, leased from Airship Industries at Cardington. It flew over a wide area, promoting Eagle Bitter, with many Wells's tenants enjoying flights. The flight path included the Greene King brewery at Biggleswade, which must have annoyed the rival company but not sufficiently to account for the later closure of the site and the concentration of Greene King's production at Bury St Edmunds. A surprise party was held for Roy Morewood to mark his 60th birthday and to celebrate the fact that Charles Wells had won sixty brewing awards over sixty years, 45 of them coming in the past ten years while Roy was in charge.

A new automatic canning line costing £1.1 million came on stream at Havelock Street in 1989. The Dragon pub in Peterborough was added to the estate, while several outlets were renovated and extended, including restoration work on a historic coaching inn, the Saracen's Head in Towcester.

1989 marked the publication of a report into the brewing industry by the government's Monopolies and Mergers Commission, a report that would have a profound impact and fundamentally change the face of brewing and retailing. The commission found that the six national brewers acted as a complex monopoly that resulted in high prices to consumers and, through the use of cheap loans and discounts, restricted independent brewers' ability to penetrate the free trade pub sector. The commission recommended that the national brewers should be restricted to a maximum of 2,000 pubs each (Allied and Bass each owned more than 7,000 pubs at the

A HOT AIR BALLOON FLIES OVER EAST ANGLIA

TO PROMOTE THE BREWERY'S PRODUCTS

time). The aim was for the pubs disposed of to become genuine free trade outlets. The commission also recommended that the tenants of Big Six breweries should have the right to buy 'guest beers' free of the tie. The publication of the report and its possible implications sent shock waves and even panic through the brewing industry at all levels. One result was that all tenants were given notice pending negotiations of new tenancy agreements while the recommendations of the report were studied.

In the long term, the MMC report and the government's Beer Orders that resulted from it proved to be, like the curate's egg, good and bad in parts. The guest beer element of the Beer Orders gave independent brewers the opportunity to sell their beers to national brewer's pubs. But the opportunities declined in step with the nationals' policy of pub disposals. The sold-off pubs did not turn into the much hoped for genuine free trade outlets but became instead part of large estates bought by restaurateurs, property companies and, increasingly, large overseas banks. The new pub companies or 'pubcos' for short were geared ruthlessly to maximising profits regardless of customers' or even tenants' interests. Such deep discounts on beer are demanded that many independent brewers cannot afford to sell beer to the pubcos. By the turn of the new century, common sense and even an awareness of consumers' interests led to greater beer choice in some of the pubco outlets, but in general it is heavily-discounted national ale and lager brands that are most commonly seen on their bars. But there has been a positive side for breweries such as Charles Wells. While the guest beer order was officially abandoned by the government in 2002, during its lifetime it did create greater consumer awareness of independent breweries and their beers.

The trading links with Mansfield Brewery intensified in 1989 with the Midland company's Riding Bitter sold in Charles Wells's pubs. The Skyship now advertised Red Stripe as well as Eagle Bitter, and Crest Lager was made available in cans to the off-licence trade. In spite of an increase in volume and turnover for the year, profits declined by a worrying 15 per cent. The trading position improved the following year, with more than 350,000 barrels of beer sold. The result was a record profit of £6,364,000 on a turnover of £66,482,000. Ten pubs were bought, including the King's Head at Bushey while the Bear in Rugby was rebuilt. Fermenting capacity was increased by purchasing 12 vessels from Whitbread following the closure of its Fremlin's Brewery in Faversham in Kent. This was part of a staged programme to double the capacity of the brewery by building a second brewhouse, with both units fully automated.

Bombardier strikes gold

Bombardier Strong Ale recorded the remarkable achievement of winning the top gold medal award at Le Monde Sélection for the fourth year running. Red Stripe spreads its wings and members of the brewing staff flew to Brisbane to train their opposite numbers at Power Brewery in producing the lager. The Red Stripe connection was cemented still further when Robert Knox, who had previously worked for Desnoes & Geddes in Jamaica, joined Charles Wells as head brewer.

The number of tied outlets increased in 1991 to an all-time record of 354 with the purchase of 43 pubs. Thirty came from Bass and five from Whitbread as the nationals set about disposing of pubs following the MMC report and the Beer Orders. The sale increased Charles Wells's presence in London and enabled an expansion into the Midlands with pubs in Coventry and Nuneaton. Peter Steer Jones retired after thirty years of brewing with the company. He did so as the brewery's turnover reached a record level of more than £79,000,000,

Red Lion, Brackley
Brian and Nigel Wiles

Brian and Nigel Wiles are a father-and-son team at the Red Lion in Brackley. The pub dates from at least 1737, when the landlord was named George Ladditt. Brackley once had 28 pubs but now has only eight. The town boasted two breweries, Brackley and Chesham, and Hopcraft and Norris.

Nigel has run the Red Lion for more than 20 years. He was a schoolboy when Brian took over the pub. In the early days, the only food sold was pork pies and sandwiches. In 1977, Brian recalls, there was no draught lager available. Ace lager was introduced but didn't sell well. Lager sales took off with the arrival of Kellerbrau. Fargo and Old Bedford barley wine were also big sellers.

Brian recalls that on the day he became the landlord the price of a pint went up by 1.5 pence. The previous tenant had held the price so Brian would get the blame. His nickname for a while was 'Brian from the Lion – his bitter's two and nine'. He sold three barrels of mild ale a week. Bitter was the second biggest seller. He also sold pint and half-pint bottles of Guinness and Mackeson, while Gold Label bottled barley wine was popular.

Nigel started work with his father in 1985 and took over the licence in 1994. Today he sells three pints of lager to one pint of bitter and his food trade is substantial.

British Rail. The additional brewhouse enabled the company to produce fourteen brews of 160 barrels each every 24 hours, creating a capacity of more than 15,000 barrels a week or 750,000 a year. To keep pace with the brewery, the office block was also extended. These exciting developments were followed in 1993 by economic depression and a flood of cheap beer from mainland Europe as the 'open borders' policy of the European Union started to make an impact. As a result of far lower duty rates in France, hordes of British day trippers went to Calais and other ports to return laden with cheap beer for home consumption. To add to the problem, the 'white van' syndrome materialised: people from all over Britain would drive to France and return with beer for illegal resale in this country. The result for Charles Wells and most other brewers was a sharp downturn in sales both in pubs and the off-trade. Against the odds, Havelock Street managed to increase production by 1 per cent as a result of orders for contract beers, but 21 pubs had to be sold and the Managed House Department was reorganised.

Deep discounting

There was further pressure on profits as the national brewers went on the rampage to increase their market share at all costs, using deep discounting in both the pub trade and in supermarkets. Nevertheless, with great optimism in the future, Charles Wells opened a new 60,000 square foot Shreeves Warehouse, named after the late Ray Shreeves, the packaging manager until his untimely death. Spending on sales and marketing was stepped up to enable the company to expand beer sales. A major sales drive was launched in London with the opening of a small warehouse at King's Cross. This Beer Courier operation set out to replace volumes of Red Stripe that had been lost as a result of the link with Bulmers. Other brands were added to make an attractive portfolio for bars in the capital.

Until 1993, Red Stripe had been the company's sole major lager brand. The lager portfolio was dramatically widened in

THIRTY-LITRE KEGS IN THE BREWERY

WAITING TO BE FILLED WITH DRAUGHT BEER

FOR ONWARD DESPATCH TO PUBS AND BARS

although profits were reduced. The Greyfriars pub in Allhallows, Bedford, built in 1959, was sold for development and a new branch of the Midland Bank was built on the site. Fittingly, given the long-standing relationship between bank and brewery, the opening ceremony was performed by Oliver Wells, who retired the following year as chairman, but stayed on as a non-executive director. His outstanding contribution to the company, to the wider brewing industry and to Bedfordshire was marked by the award of an OBE in the Queen's Honours. John Wells took over as chairman and managing director. James Baker and Jonathan Harrison retired and were replaced by Ian McNicholl as finance director and Laurie Clark as tied trade director.

This was a year of yet more growth and development at the brewery. The second brewhouse was completed, with an opening ceremony carried out by Sir Peter Parker, the industrialist best known for his ebullient chairmanship of

BOTTLES SPEED ROUND THE ULTRA-MODERN

PACKAGING HALL. THE END PRODUCTS ARE

SOLD IN BRITAIN, NORTH AMERICA, MAINLAND

EUROPE, RUSSIA AND THE BALTIC

Beers full of Eastern promise

The most fascinating Kirin beer brewed under licence by Charles Wells is Ichiban, which means Number One or simply Best. The 5.5% beer is made from the 'first runnings' of the mash vessel. Full saccharification or conversion of starch to sugar takes place but the sugary extract or wort is not 'sparged' – this means the mash does not get a final rinse with hot brewing liquor to wash out any remaining sugars. The wort from two separate mashes are blended and then boiled with hops and fermented. The finished beer has a full, biscuity aroma and flavour balanced by floral hops.

The acclaimed German Pilsner Bitburger was also added to the portfolio, but this beer was factored, not brewed under licence. An opportunity arose in the mid-1990s to brew a new lager with a quite different heritage to either the Caribbean or Japan. Roy Morewood was approached by a company keen to brew and sell an Indian lager in Britain called Cobra. Roy said Charles Wells could only contemplate taking on such a contract if volumes of 10,000 barrels a year could be achieved. John Wells then met the founder of the company, Karan Bilimoria, who explained he wanted, in effect, a draught beer in bottle with a lower gas content than most packaged beers. This would make the beer easier and smoother to drink, and an ideal companion for Asian food.

Head Brewer Jim Robertson looked at the version of Cobra brewed in Mysore in India and devised a recipe suitable for Britain. 10,000 barrels were brewed in 1997 and Cobra now accounts for 60,000 barrels a year. It is the biggest-selling Indian beer in Britain and is exported to Europe, the United States and even to India.

BOTH MODERN AND TRADITIONAL IMAGES ARE USED TO PROMOTE KIRIN AND COBRA LAGERS, BREWED UNDER LICENCE AT BEDFORD BUT BASED STRICTLY ON ORIGINAL RECIPES

1993 when an agreement was reached to brew the Japanese Kirin brands under licence. The first contact had been made with Kirin in the early 1990s by Alec Monk, one of the company's non-executive directors. John Wells and Roy Morewood then visited Japan. An earthquake took place while they were there, an inauspicious start to relations with the Japanese. But Charles Wells was determined to forge a business relationship with a company that was one of the top ten breweries in the world and has a massive presence in its home market. In 1993 Alec Monk and John Wells, then chairman of Charles Wells, went to Japan and returned with an agreement that stipulated that the Japanese had to be satisfied with the quality of the beer brewed in Bedford. Roy Morewood says he was questioned intensively by Kirin technicians for several weeks. He says they took copious notes, went into 'unbelievable' detail and remembered every single word from countless meetings and discussions.

The current head brewer, Jim Robertson, who is Roy Morewood's son-in-law, has a copy of the Kirin Blue Book that lays down in minute detail every part of the brewing process.

Kirin is the oldest brewery in Japan, and its name and logo are based on a mythical creature that is half deer and half dragon. Its main Pilsner-style lager is highly regarded throughout the world. With a Japanese brewer based at Bedford to check quality, Kirin is brewed with malted barley, maize and rice, and is hopped with Czech Saaz for aroma and German Northern Brewer for bitterness.

Roy Morewood retired in 1993 and became a non-executive director. His role as head brewer and technical director had been a remarkable one, steering the brewery through its innovative and daring changes in the late 1970s from traditional ale brewery in Horne Lane to the modern and flexible new site at Havelock Street. He was also at the centre of the company's drive into Europe, devising beers more suitable for continental tastes, such as Crest Pils, a 10 per cent Super Crest, a strong export version of Bombardier, and a version of Old Bedford Ale marketed as Eagle Export. The widespread view in the brewing industry was that British ale and pubs were so intrinsically 'English' that they could not flourish abroad. Charles Wells had a different perspective and

by 1996 it had 44 branded pubs in Italy, seven in Spain and one in France. Overseas sales made an important contribution to company profits.

Paul Wells joined the board in 1991 as national accounts sales director. He became sales and marketing director and deputy managing director in 1994. Aileen Wells died in 1994. She had been the first female director of a brewery when she joined the company in 1947 to represent the trust created by her father, Ernest Wells. In a full and rewarding life, she was a Red Cross officer during World War Two. In that capacity she went on a mission to Odessa in 1945 in the troop ship Duchess of Richmond to bring home British prisoners-of-war. After the war she was active in the Red Cross in Bedfordshire, holding every senior post in the organisation, including that of Patron. She was one of the first women to be appointed a Deputy Lord Lieutenant of an English county. She retired from all activities in 1989 as a result of ill health and was nursed at her home, The Tofte, Sharnbrooke, and then in a nursing home in Milton Ernest, where she died.

The emphasis on European sales did not result in any slackening of emphasis on the home front. In 1994, beer volumes increased and for the first time exceeded 500,000 barrels. The Queen's Arms in Draycott Avenue in London's South Kensington district was bought from Scottish & Newcastle as part of a trading agreement that saw McEwan's lager sold in Wells's pubs.

Quenching festival thirsts

The brewery became the sponsor of the Cambridge Folk Festival, the biggest event of its kind in the country. The festival draws large crowds that eagerly sup some 100,000 pints of Eagle, Bombardier and Red Stripe. A purpose-built bar measuring one hundred feet in length was commissioned to serve thirsty festival-goers as fast as possible. The bar became a fixture and hallmark at the festival in successive years. The brewery also became involved in the Bedfordshire Festival at Old Warden, an important event that attracted thousands of visitors over the three-day August Bank Holiday weekend. Charles Wells became a joint sponsor of the festival with Jordans Cereals and set up an on-site pub called the Shuttleworth Arms. Draught Fargo was re-launched at the festival in 1994. The brand had been withdrawn for several years as a result of a dispute, now settled, between the brewery and the Wells Fargo Bank in the United States.

The first Charles Wells pub abroad was opened near Florence in Italy in 1980. Charles Wells was now trading with ten of the twelves states of the European Union, and also in North America. The annual report that year claimed that the company was now one of the top three producers of beer in Britain outside the ranks of the national brewers. Turnover for the year was a record £88 million but the difficulties of trading at the time as a result of intense competition as well as the investment in marketing made a small profit possible only by the sale of pubs that brought in £300,000.

The mid-1990s saw the retirement of Toby Dobson, with Roger Ashworth taking over from Ian McNicholl and joining the board as finance director. Nigel McNally, who was to play a leading role in driving sales of beer in the free trade in the 1990s, joined the company as marketing manager.

By early 1995, the house magazine Pint Pot reported that annual production was running at 550,000 barrels. Talks were held with Anglia Water in order that the brewery could draw more brewing liquor from its well. A national Chalkboard publicity campaign was launched on posters and on television in a bid to bring the company's brands to the attention of a wider audience. This included a Chalk and Cheers promotion that offered free pints to pub customers and collector coupons to win prizes. Such initiatives were urgently needed, as beer volumes declined by 2.9 per cent that year. The Beer Courier service based at King's Cross expanded by taking over routes from Whitbread's delivery company that had the rather inelegant title of Glug Beer.

Charles Wells held talks with the Mexican brewer Grupo Modelo, which led to Wells being given the exclusive rights to import and distribute Corona Extra, a lager best known for

THE CAMBRIDGE FOLK FESTIVAL (LEFT AND BELOW) HAS A SPECIAL BAR WHERE WELLS'S BEERS ARE SERVED. RIGHT, A 2003 GATHERING OF THE WELLS FAMILY FROM BRITAIN AND ABROAD WITH PAUL WELLS EXTREME RIGHT

IN 1980, THE ANNUAL

REPORT CLAIMED THE

COMPANY WAS TRADING

WITH 10 OF THE 12

STATES OF THE EU

being drunk by its aficionados straight from the bottle with a slice of lime placed in the neck. The company's success with Corona was instrumental in helping it to build an expanded national sales structure.

Michael Cottrell, who joined the board as a non-executive director in 1995, and with a long and distinguished career in the brewing industry, died suddenly the following year. Nigel McNally, the head of marketing, became marketing director at a time of some difficulty for the company. Volumes declined by a worrying 12 per cent while a new high-speed, 'state of the art' bottling line costing £1.5 million failed to perform. The tied estate was reduced to 297. Although turnover was reduced, a small increase in net profit was achieved, thanks in part to buoyant sales in Europe. Recognition of Charles Wells's European initiatives was rewarded in 1997 when the company was presented with the coveted Queen's Award for Export. A bottled extra-strong version of Bombardier, called

Celebration Ale, was brewed to mark the award, and a Bombardier Bar in Paris was opened, underscoring the importance of the brand to the company in both domestic and overseas markets.

The year saw considerable activity at board level. John Wells stood down as chairman and managing director after 29 years with the company but stayed on as a non-executive director. Tom Wells was appointed vice chairman and wines and spirits director, with Paul Wells becoming managing director. The strong family ties with the company were strengthened when Peter Wells, son of John and great-great-grandson of the founder, became on trade marketing manager. Anthony Wallis joined the board as free trade director, while Alec Monk, a non-executive director for nine years, became the first person from outside the family to become chairman.

A 35 per cent stake in the McKenzie Group added two live music venues, the Shepherds Bush Empire and the Brixton

GOD REST YE
MERRY ENGLISHMEN

SPIFFINGLY ENGLISH

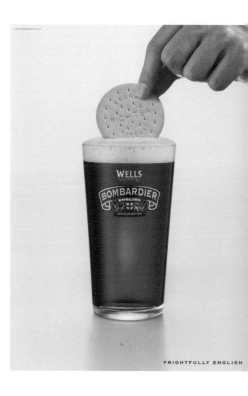

FRIGHTFULLY ENGLISH

Academy, to Charles Wells's outlets. A joint venture with Route 8 supported the opening of a new London restaurant, R&K Stanley's in Little Portland Street.

John Gibbs, the business development manager, retired in 1998 after 36 years with the brewery. He joined Charles Wells in 1963 after twelve years' service in the Royal Navy. In 1997, John and wife, Stella, were invited to meet Prince Charles at a garden party at Highgrove where they were thanked for their work with The Prince's Trust.

The problems of trading and declining profits were addressed by the board in 1998. The result was a decision to withdraw from own-label canned beers for supermarkets: this sector was so fiercely competitive, with the national brewers discounting their products as 'loss leaders', that Charles Wells's products could make only minimal profits. Five hotels and thirty pubs were sold in a further bid to boost income. The pub estate numbered 292 outlets as a result.

The policy worked well. By 1999, contract brewing and packaging increased, and net profits recorded an increase from the low of the previous year. A corporate design featuring a new logo, lettering and colour were introduced for brands, pubs and transport. Trading was still difficult, however. The government's Beer Orders meant that the national brewers were now concentrating their attack on the free trade and independent brewers' pubs, where they sold beer at massive discounts in order to corner the 'guest beer' market. Small rural pubs were badly affected and Charles Wells decided to restructure its estate. As a result, forty managed houses were transferred to tenancies while fifty tenanted pubs were sold, reducing the total pub estate to 254. Some 50,000 visitors to the Millennium Bedfordshire Festival drank 35,000 pints of ale and lager in the Shuttleworth Arms. In an attempt to open the take-home market to cask ale, Charles Wells developed four-pint PET bottles for Eagle and Bombardier: the beer was unfiltered and appealed to real ale drinkers. The PETs were replaced the following year by vented mini-casks of Bombardier in attractive, cask-shaped containers.

JOHN BULL FINEST BITTER IS A NEW CASK BEER INTRODUCED IN 2004 FOR THE DOMESTIC MARKET

BY GEORGE,
LET'S CELEBRATE

JOLLY ENGLISH

REALLY RATHER ENGLISH

A BEER FOR ALL MOODS AND ALL SEASONS...THESE NEW IMAGES FOR BOMBARDIER SHOW THAT CHARLES WELLS HAS NOW BECOME THE SHORTER, SNAPPIER 'WELLS'

Charles Wells entered a new century and new millennium in good heart and with sound finances. It began the year 2000 by buying the John Bull 28-strong pub franchise chain from Allied Domecq. This gave the company new outlets in Russia and the Baltic States. The export business accounted for 20 per cent of beer volumes, with forty themed bars in Europe and the East serving Charles Wells' ales and lagers. As a result of the deal with Allied Domecq, Charles Wells brews John Bull Bitter for export. In 2003, it bought the exclusive rights to the brand for export sales and ultimately for the home market as well. Twenty-six years after the first brew of Red Stripe in Britain, Charles Wells became solely responsible for sales and marketing of the brand in Britain, rights previously held by Bulmers which was later bought by Scottish & Newcastle.

In 2004, Wells launched John Bull in cask-conditioned form for the domestic market. The beer was first brewed by Paines of St Neots and was later bought by the national Allied Breweries group, which promoted it as a keg brand for pubs in London and the South-east. The Well's cask version uses pale

Water: it's good enough to bottle

In 2004, Charles Wells received confirmation that its brewing water is of the highest quality, so good in fact that it could be bottled and sold as mineral water. It was the supply of water that founder Charles Wells was at great pains to secure, piping it some distance from its source at Park Road to Horne Lane. Additional piping was laid to continue to pump the same supply to the new brewery in Havelock Street.

Working with hydro-geologists, the Environment Agency and Bedford Borough Council, the brewery was told that its water or 'brewing liquor' was so pure and with such a fine balance of natural salts that would be granted mineral water status. As far as the brewery is aware, it is the only British brewer with such a seal of quality for its water.

Water makes up 90% of even the strongest beer and its composition brings out the best qualities from malt and hops. Soft water is needed for lager brewing, while hard water, with gypsum and magnesium, is favoured for ale brewing. The water is adjusted in the brewery to suit particular styles of beer.

ale and crystal malts with English hop varieties. They combine to produce a beer with a fine balance of juicy malt, tart and bitter hops and tangy citrus fruit.

Pub trading remains a tough business. The Beer Orders had the opposite result to the recommendations of the Monopolies and Mergers Commission. Today, four international brewers – Scottish & Newcastle, Interbrew, Coors and Carlsberg – dominate the British market and account for eight out of every ten pints of beer brewed. Bass and Whitbread left brewing in 2000, their brands and breweries divided between Coors and Interbrew. The close trading links between the national brewers and the new breed of pub companies, based upon massive discounting, saw 44 breweries close in the 1990s, unable to compete with the nationals. Wolverhampton & Dudley and Greene King, two public companies, are the only large regional brewers with pub estates to have survived.

Charles Wells, second in size to W&D and Greene King, enjoys a unique position in Britain as the only substantial regional brewer with national distribution that is still owned by its founding family. The decision to develop its brands, take on contract brewing and packaging, along with the drive into Europe, has allowed the company to flourish and build powerful buffers against the national brewers.

Charles Wells would not recognise the industry or even the brewery he founded more than 125 years ago. But he would marvel at the success of the modern company and the broad sweep of its activities. Above all, he would feel a warm glow of pride at the fact that the fourth and fifth generations of his family are firmly in control of his 'tight ship' and are determined to guide it to further success in the years ahead.

THE IMPRESSIVE NEW EAGLE CENTRE (RIGHT)
AT HAVELOCK STREET, CAPTURED AT NIGHT.
THE BUILDING INCLUDES A BAR, RESTAURANT,
MEETING ROOMS, WITH TRAINING FACILITIES
FOR TENANTS AND MANAGERS.
THE COMPANY WAS GIVEN A MAJOR BOOST
WHEN IT WON THE QUEEN'S AWARD
FOR EXPORT ACHIEVEMENT IN 1997

ELIZABETH THE SECOND,

by the Grace of God of the United Kingdom of Great Britain and Northern Ireland and of Our other Realms and Territories Queen, Defender of the Faith, to

Charles Wells Limited

Greeting!

We being cognisant of the outstanding achievement of the said body as manifested in the furtherance and increase of the Export Trade of Our United Kingdom of Great Britain and Northern Ireland, Our Channel Islands and Our Island of Man and being desirous of showing Our Royal Favour do hereby confer upon it

THE QUEEN'S AWARD FOR EXPORT ACHIEVEMENT

for a period of five years from the twenty-first day of April 1997 until the twentieth day of April 2002 and do hereby give permission for the authorised flag of the said Award to be flown during that time by the said body and for the device thereof to be displayed in the manner authorised by Our Warrant of t...

IDYLLIC SETTINGS FOR WELLS'S
RURAL PUBS. THE ANCHOR INN
STANDS ALONGSIDE THE RIVER
AT GREAT BARFORD WHILE THE
WHITE HORSE, BEDFORD, FEATURES
AN ELEGANT DINING ROOM

Charles Wells public houses
November 2004

Admiral Vernon 31 High Street, Over, Cambs

Anchor Inn The Square, Aspley Guise, Milton Keynes, Bucks

Anchor Inn High Street Great Barford, Beds

Anchor and Hope 36 The Cut, Waterloo, London SE1

Anglers Rest Clapham Road, Bedford, Beds

Ashwell Arms Ashwell Street, Leighton Buzzard, Beds

Banbury Cross 7 Butchers Row, Banbury, Oxon

Bar Citrus 29 Harpur Street, Bedford, Beds

Barley Mow 42 Main Street,Hartford, Huntingdon, Cambs

Bat and Barrel 104-106 Park Street, Luton, Beds

Bear Bilton Lane, Long Lawford, Rugby, Warks

Bedford Arms 64 High Street, Toddington, Beds

Bedford Arms High Street, Oakley, Beds

Bedford Arms 2 Bromham Road, Bedford, Beds

Beehive 22 The Green, Deanshanger, Milton Keynes, Bucks

Beehive Beehive Lane, Welwyn Garden City, Herts

Bell Inn Gt. North Road, Eaton Socon, Cambs

Binley Oak Paynes Lane, Coventry, Warks

Bird-In-Hand 117 Brickhill Drive, Bedford, Beds

Blacksmiths Arms 1 Downs Barn Boulevard, Downs Barn, Milton Keynes, Bucks

Blarney Stone Roise Street, Bedford, Beds

Boot 110 High Street, Langford, Beds

Bramingham Quantock Rise, Bramingham Park, Luton, Beds

Branagans The Hollow, Earl Shilton, Leics

Bricklayers Arms 29 Queens Street, Hitchin, Herts

Bridge 50 High Street, Shefford, Beds

Bull 9 Market Place, Olney, Bucks

Burnaby Arms, 66 Stanley Street, Bedford, Beds

Bushel & Strike, Mill Street, Ashwell, Herts

Cambs Hunter Berkeley Street, Eynesbury, St Neots, Cambs

Carpenters Arms The High Street, Cranfield, Beds

Castle Newnham Street, Bedford, Beds

Chase Coleshill Road, Chapel End, Nuneaton, Warks

Chequers 26 Lutterworth Road, Burbage, Hinckley, Leics

Chequers Hall End, Wootton, Beds

Cherry Tree Sheep Street, Market Square, Kettering, Northants

Circuit Bar 13 St Paul's Square, Bedford, Beds

Coach and Horses Oxford Street, Wellingborough, Northants

Cock Inn 16 High Street, North Crawley, Bucks

Cock Inn 2 Bedford Road, Wootton, Beds

Compasses 44 High Street, Greenfield, Beds

Corner House 117/119 Tavistock Street, Bedford, Beds

Corner House Market Square, St Neots, Cambs

Countryman Bradwell Common Boulevard, Milton Keynes, Bucks

Cricketers Arms 107 Arlesey Rd, Ickleford, Near Hitchin, Herts

Cross Keys Newport Road, Great Woolstone, Milton Keynes, Bucks

Cross Keys 13 High Street, Pulloxhill, Beds

Crown Inn Main Street, Tingewick, Bucks

Crown & Pipes High Street, Fenstanton, Huntingdon, Cambs

Cuba Hotel Newport Road, New Bradwell, Milton Keynes, Bucks

Cuckoo 120 High Street, Wollaston, Wellingborough, Northants

Daniel Defoe 102 Church Street, Stoke Newington, London N16

De Parys Hotel De Parys Avenue, Bedford, Beds

Devonshire Arms 32 Dudley Street, Bedford, Beds

Dobblers Inn 184 Sturton Street, Cambridge, Cambs

Dog And Duck Parkside Drive, Houghton Regis, Beds

Dog & Partridge Titchmarsh, Nr Kettering, Northants

Dolphin East Street, Stamford, Lincs

Dolphin 134 Main Road, Middleton Cheyney, Banbury, Oxon

Dolphin Whaddon Way, Bletchley, Milton Keynes, Bucks

Dolphin High Street, Newport Pagnell, Bucks

Double Four The Ringway, Rothersthorpe Road, Northampton, Northants

Dragon Hodgson Centre, Werrington, Peterborough, Cambs

Dragoon 18 Buckden Road, Brampton, Cambs

Druids Napier Street Cambridge, Cambs

Duck on the Pond The Green, Long Itchington, Warks

Duke Inn 10 Woburn Road, Kempston, Beds

Duke of Edinburgh 3 Adelaide Street, Northampton, Northants

Eaton Oak Crosshall Road, Eaton Ford, St Neots, Cambs

Elephant and Castle Aldermans Green Road, Coventry, Warks

Elm Tree Orchard Street, Cambridge, Cambs

Embankment Hotel The Embankment, Bedford, Beds

Falcon Inn Rushden Road, Bletsoe, Beds

Feathers High Street, Rushden, Northants

THE GARDEN OF THE BEDFORD ARMS, OAKLEY (LEFT).

THE COCK, NORTH CRAWLEY (BELOW).

THE FORESTERS ARMS, BEDFORD (RIGHT)

Fir Tree Hotel The Square, Woburn Sands, Bucks

Fleur-De-Lis Mill Street, Bedford, Beds

Folly Inn London Road, Towcester, Northampton, Northants

Foresters Arms Union Street, Bedford, Beds

Foresters Arms Newport Road, New Bradwell, Bucks

Foundry Arms Victoria Road, Fenny Stratford, Milton Keynes, Bucks

Fox Inn Bakers Lane, Farthinghoe, Brackley, Northants

Fox Inn Thorpe Waterville, Kettering, Northants

Fox & Hounds Milton Road, Clapham, Beds

Fox & Hounds High Street, Riseley, Beds

George Inn Harborough Road, Brixworth, Northants

Globe Inn Huntingdon Street, St Neots, Cambs

Gloucester Arms Gloucester Road, Bedford, Beds

Golden Lion 498 Goldington Road, Bedford, Beds

Golden Pheasant 71 High Street, Biggleswade, Beds

Gordon Arms 118 Castle Road, Bedford, Beds

Green Dragon 1 Hall Hill, Brigstock, Corby, Northants

Green Man Lower Tachbrook Street, Leamington Spa, Warks

Greyhound 41 Crowland Road, Eye Green, Peterborough, Cambs

Guinea Bedford Road, Moggerhanger, Beds

Half Moon High Street, Kempston, Beds

Half Moon 42 Main Road, Grendon, Northants

Hare & Hounds High Street, Great Addington, Kettering, Northants

Hare & Hounds The Village, Old Warden, Biggleswade, Beds

Headlands Longland Road, Northampton, Northants

Horseshoe High Street, Lavendon, Near Olney, Bucks

Horseshoes High Street, Blunham, Beds

H.G.'S 10 Queen Street, Peterborough, Cambs

Jackal 3 High Street, Thurleigh, Beds

Jailhouse Much Park Street, Coventry, Warks

Jolly Coopers Ward Hedges, Flitton, Beds

Jolly Sailor Stonecross, St Albans, Herts

King Edward 158 Queens Street, Rushden, Northants

King of Denmark 7/9 Cloudesley Road, London N1

King William IV 56 High Street, Kempston, Beds

Kings Arms Tickford Street, Newport Pagnell, Bucks

Kings Head Little Bushey Lane, Bushey, Herts

Lamb Inn Orlingbury Road, Little Harrowden, Northants

Leathern Bottel Newport Road, Wavendon, Milton Keynes, Bucks

Leeds Arms The Green, Eltisley, St Neots, Cambs

Lord Roberts 1 Market Square, Sandy, Beds

Magpie 54 High Street, Harrold, Beds

THE NEW SUN INN, KIMBOLTON (ABOVE).

THE PARK, BEDFORD (RIGHT)

Marquis of Anglesey 77 Ashmill Street, London NW1

Mason Arms Huntingdon Road, Thrapston, Kettering, Northants

Mill Hotel 32/34 Mill Street, Bedford, Beds

Moorings Myton Road, Leamington Spa, Warks

Mulberry Bush Southfield Centre, Kempston, Beds

Nags Head 44 Midland Road, Bedford, Beds

Nags Head Greenfield Road, Westoning, Beds

Nags Head Queens Road, Nuneaton, Warks

Narrowboat Watling Street, Weedon, Northampton, Northants

Neptune Werrington Street, Euston, London

New Bowling Green 13 St Nicholas, Church Street, Warwick, Warks

New Inn 2 Bradwell Road, New Bradwell, Milton Keynes, Bucks

New Sun Inn 20 High Street, Kimbolton, Cambs

New Zealand 175 Buckingham Road, Aylesbury, Bucks

Nightingale Peregrine Way, Langford Village, Bicester, Oxon

North Western Hotel Stratford Road, Wolverton, Bucks

Oak Tree 15 Leyton Green, Harpenden, Herts

Oakley Arms 98 High Street, Harrold, Beds

Oddfellows Arms Main Street, Higham on the Hill, Nuneaton, Warks

Oddfellows Arms Upper Abbey Street, Nuneaton, Warks

Old Cherry Tree Cherry Tree Lane, Great Houghton, Northampton, Northants

Old Crown Inn 1 Stoke Road, Ashton, Northants

Old Globe 191 Mile End Road, London, London E1

Old King Johns Head 90 Whiston Road, Kingsland, London E2

Old Red Lion 12 The Green, Clipston, Market Harborough, Leics

Olde Kings Arms 41 High Street, Old Town, Hemel Hempstead, Herts

Park 98 Kimbolton Road, Bedford, Beds

Pheasant 300 Kimbolton Road, Bedford, Beds

Phoenix 45 St Johns Street, Bedford, Beds

Plough Leverstock Green, Hemel Hempstead, Herts

Plough London Road, Stoney Stratford, Milton Keynes, Bucks

Plough High Street, Newport Pagnell, Bucks

Plough Inn Shutlanger, Near Towcester, Northants

Plough Inn 196 Watling Street, Towcester, Northants

Plough Inn Aynho Road, Adderbury, Banbury, Oxon

Pomfret Arms Vernon Road, Towcester, Northants

Prince Albert Vicarage Road, Bradwell Village, Milton Keynes, Bucks

Prince of Wales 42 Croyland Road, Wellingborough, Northants

Prince of Wales Northampton Road, Bromham, Beds

Prince of Wales 24 Bedford Street, Ampthill, Beds

Punchbowl Tuttle Hill, Nuneaton, Warks

Queen 36 Preston Road, Bedford, Beds

Queen Victoria 10 High Street, Gayton, Blisworth, Northants

Queens Head Woburn Street, Ampthill, Beds

Queens Head The Lane, Tebworth, Near Leighton Buzzard, Beds

Railway Tavern 399 Mare Street, Hackney, London E8

Railway Tavern 3 East Barnet Road, New Barnet, Herts

Ranelagh Ranelagh Road, Wellingborough, Northants

Red Lion Bedford Road, Wilstead, Beds

Red Lion 89 High Street, Yardley Hastings, Northants

Red Lion 11 Market Place, Brackley, Northants

Red Lion Main Street, Denton, Northants

Red Lion Hotel Wavendon Road, Salford, Milton Keynes, Bucks

Red Lion Hotel Main Street, East Haddon, Northants

Rising Sun Sun Street, Biggleswade, Beds

Rising Sun 11 Everton Road, Potton, Beds

Romer Arms The Green, Newnham Village, Daventry, Northants

Rose & Crown 171 Bedford Road, Marston Moretaine, Beds

Rose & Crown Silver Street, Newport Pagnell, Bucks

Rose & Crown 89 High Street, Ridgmont, Beds

Royal Exchange 2 High Street, Leamington Spa, Warks

Royal George 57 High Street, Stagsden, Beds

Royal Oak 42 Sparrow Herne, Bushey Herts

Royal Oak Bridgend, Carlton, Beds

Royal Oak Oldbury Road, Hartshill, Nuneaton, Warks

Royal Oak High Street, Hail Weston, St Neots, Cambs

Royal Oak Church Street, Lidlington, Beds

Royal Oak High Street, Houghton Conquest, Beds

Royal Oak High Street, Roxton, Beds

Salisbury Arms Tenison Road, Cambridge, Cambs

Saracens Head Ricksford Hill, Aylesbury, Bucks

Seven Stars Albert Square, Rugby, Warks

Ship Northfield Avenue, Cambridge, Cambs

Ship Inn 102 Bromham Road, Bedford, Beds

Shoulder of Mutton Brookside, Stretton on Dunsmore, Rugby, Warks

Silver Cup St Albans Road, Harpenden, Herts

Smiths Arms 15 Margetts Road, Kempston, Beds

Social 33 Linton Street, London N1

Somerstown Coffee House 60 Chalton Street, London NW1

Sondes Arms Main Street, Rockingham, Near Market Harborough, Leics

Southend Ampthill Road, Bedford, Beds

Sportsman 58 The Boundary, Bedford, Beds

Spread Eagle 147 Wellingborough Road, Northampton, Northants

St Ives Motel London Road, St Ives, Cambs

Stags Head High Street, Earlsbarton, Northants

Stag Inn Mentmore, Near Leighton Buzzard, Beds

Star 42 High Street, Clapham, Beds

Star 10 High Street, Wellingborough, Northants

Star & Garter The Green, Chelveston, Wellingborough, Northants

Sun Inn 126 High Street, Broughton, Northants

Sun Inn Grange Road, Felmersham, Beds

Swan High Street, Sherington, Newport Pagnell, Bucks

Swan 3 High Street, Clapham, Beds

Swan Inn 1 Winslow Road, Great Horwood, Bucks

Swan Inn 1 Dunstable Road, Flitwick, Beds

Swan Inn High Street, Offord Cluny, St Neots, Cambs

Swan Inn Felmersham Road, Radwell, Beds

Swan with Two Nicks High Street, Sharnbrook, Beds

Talbot 5 North Street, Stilton, Peterborough, Cambs

Territorial High Street, Huntingdon, Cambs

Three Compasses Upper Dean, Huntingdon, Cambs

Tollemache Arms High Street, Harrington, Northants

Plough Simpson Village, Milton Keynes, Bucks

Turnpike 139 Eastcotts Road, Bedford, Beds

Victoria 110 Grove Road, Bow, London E3

Viking Grangeway Home Farm Estate, Rushden, Northants

Vine 4 South Green, Coates, Cambs

Vine 19 Church Street, Market Deeping, Lincs

Vivian Arms Knox Road, Wellingborough, Northants

Waggon and Horses Bedford Road, Barton-Le-Clay, Beds

Waggon and Horses Kettering Road, Burton Latimer, Northants

Watts Arms Castlethorpe Road, Hanslope, Near Wolverton, Milton Keynes, Bucks

Wellington 16 Bedford Road, Kempston, Beds

Wentworth Arms 127 Eric Street, Mile End, London E3

Wheatsheaf Station Road, Bow Brickhill, Milton Keynes, Bucks

Wheatsheaf 15 High Street, Flitwick, Beds

Wheatsheaf 185 Baker Street, Enfield, Middlesex

Wheatsheaf Great North Road, Eaton Socon, Cambs

Wheatsheaf Mount Pleasant, Aspley Guise, Bucks

White Hart Streatley Road, Upper Sundon, Beds

White Hart High Street, Stoke Goldington, Bucks

White Horse High Street, Tilbrook, Kimbolton, Cambs

White Horse 101 Station Road, Flitwick, Beds

White Horse 49 Nelson Street, Market Harborough, Leics

White Horse Kimbolton Road, Keysoe, Beds

White Horse 84 Newnham Avenue, Bedford, Beds

White Horse Inn Daventry Road, Norton, Near Daventry, Northants

White Lion North Street, Leighton Buzzard, Beds

White Swan All Saints Square, Bedworth, Warks

Windmill Charlton, Near Hitchin, Herts

Windsor Castle 12 Albert Road, Luton, Beds

Woolpack 35 Church Street, St Neots, Cambs

Wrestlers 337 Newmarket Road, Cambridge, Cambs

OLD RED LION, CLIPSTON (ABOVE).

RED LION, SALFORD (RIGHT)

Picture sources

Mark Turner: all colour photographs of public houses,
the Eagle Brewery, Charles Wells staff and stills photography.

Archive photographs: Charles Wells, members of the Wells family,
and members of the staff.

Bedfordshire and Luton Archives and Records Service:
pages 21, 26 (right), 27 (top), 29 (bottom), 62/63, 86/87.

Felix Man / Getty Images: page 84 (left).

Imperial War Museum: page 60.

Mike Wells: page 85 (aircraft piloted by Oliver Wells).

National Portrait Gallery: page 22.

Nick Elliott Music Photographer: page 106 (right).

Phil Dent / Redferns: page 106 (left).